Truth, Love and Immortality

Truth, Love and Immortality

An Introduction to McTaggart's Philosophy

P. T. Geach

University of California Press

Berkeley and Los Angeles

University of California Press
Berkeley and Los Angeles

© P. T. Geach 1979

ISBN 0-520-03755-3

Library of Congress Catalog Card Number 78-62842

Printed in Great Britain

Contents

The longer I live, the more I am convinced of the reality of three things – truth, love and immortality.

MCTAGGART

Preface

My first acknowledgement of indebtedness must be to my father, Professor G. H. Geach; he had the good fortune to have McTaggart as his director of studies at Cambridge. My father was my first teacher of philosophy; it was he who induced me to read McTaggart, and I had many valuable discussions of McTaggart's philosophy with him.

Next, I have to thank the trustees of St Deiniol's Library, Hawarden, for awarding me a Gladstone Research Studentship for the academic year 1938–9, which enabled me to devote a year's research to McTaggart. The Polish Academy of Sciences kindly invited me to read a paper on McTaggart's idealism, in the spring of 1968; this paper, '*Konsekwentny idealizm?*' ('A consequent idealism?'), was published in *Studia Filozoficzne* in 1969. Finally, I am most grateful for the generous permission given me by the University of Pennsylvania to choose McTaggart's philosophy as the subject of my seminar during my visit in the spring of 1970, although it was clear that only a few students would be attending.

When I first read Professor Broad's *Examination of McTaggart's Philosophy* forty or so years ago, I formed no favourable view of it; the passing years have made me change my mind about many things, but not about this. I can here acknowledge no indebtedness, except that I have seen some pitfalls that an expositor must avoid. This laborious work seems to me neither to capture the spirit of McTaggart's philosophy nor to be reliable in detail. In my own book I refer to Broad's commentary only for some of its more important misinterpretations and misconceived criticisms.

The MSS of McTaggart's *Nature of Existence*, vol. 2, from which Broad worked, have not been found; but some detective work by Dr C. Lewy revealed that Mrs McTaggart had deposited in Trinity College a complete MS of vol. 2, Draft A, together with notes for the preparation of Draft B, and I was kindly allowed to study this. I am most grateful to Dr Lewy and to the Librarian. The most important thing in this MS, to my mind, is the evidence it affords about McTaggart's views on Matter: I have added a note on this to my chapter on the topic.

For the biographical information in the Introduction, and for the saying of McTaggart that appears on page 6, I am indebted to the biography of McTaggart by Lowes Dickinson (Cambridge University Press, 1931).

Chapter 1 originally formed a Stanton Lecture that I delivered in Cambridge in 1971.

Readers who have not a special interest in the theory of groups and wholes may pass over some of the discussion at the beginning of Chapter 5 (pages 62–7).

Like the Tichborne Claimant, whom he resembled in physique, McTaggart comes into court with heavy prejudice against him. The jurymen know of him as a fabricator of paradoxes; his denial of the reality of time is notorious, and they will have a vague but quite correct impression that there are many other paradoxes involved in his claims. The only hope of the case's being presented and judged fairly is that a commentator should not obtrude his own philosophical position but should state McTaggart's as clearly and sympathetically as he can; I have tried to observe this principle. My readers must therefore understand, once for all: I state theses and arguments of McTaggart's without raising objections I am not to be taken as accepting them; my agreement is not to be assumed unless I explicitly say I agree with McTaggart. Counsel is not vouching for his client's being right in fact or law; but the client is an honest man and has a right to a fair hearing.

P. T. Geach
University of Leeds
All Souls' Day, 1977

Introduction

McTaggart's life

In spite of his name, McTaggart's family was not Scottish but deep-rootedly English: both his father and his mother, who were in fact first cousins, came from an old Wiltshire stock of yeoman farmers surnamed Ellis. In the eighteenth century some of the family turned from farming to trade with the West Indies. In the early nineteenth century Thomas Flower Ellis, McTaggart's grandfather, was a distinguished QC and a Fellow of the Royal Society; his son Francis Ellis, McTaggart's father, was also a distinguished lawyer, who became a County Court judge at an early age. Thomas Flower Ellis had married Susan McTaggart, sister of a Scottish baronet, Sir John McTaggart: the future philosopher was given the forenames 'John McTaggart' after his great-uncle. When Sir John died without heirs, he left money to his nephew Francis Ellis upon condition that he should take the additional surname of McTaggart; so our hero became John McTaggart Ellis McTaggart, and always used this remarkable style in full on the title-pages of his books.

McTaggart was born on Cromwell's 'lucky' day, 3 September, in 1866: he took pleasure in the date of his birth, and the choice of examples in his books betrays an admiration for Cromwell, such as many Englishmen have felt whom one cannot remotely imagine living happily under that sort of dictatorial régime. His father died in 1870: in 1872 his mother, to whom he was extremely devoted all his life, settled in Weybridge, Surrey, where she remained till 1890. McTaggart showed a bent for abstract thought extremely early in life; the story is told of him, as it is of Aquinas, that as a young child he would wander around thinking about God.

McTaggart grew up in an atmosphere of Victorian liberalism

and atheism. He had to be removed from his first preparatory school because in conversation with the other boys he denied the existence of God and set about disproving the articles of the Apostles' Creed. Things went better at his next school, in Caterham. Here he was generally regarded as mad by his contemporaries: extreme untidiness and absent-mindedness, utter incompetence at football, and an expression of interest in philosophy, are a sufficient explanation. He does not seem to have been specially unhappy; and his speculative interests had already by now turned to Kant.

In 1882 McTaggart became a boarder at Clifton College. He was the sort of boy who was bound to suffer much from such a school. He was again too honest, and too little worldly-wise, to deny or even conceal the atheistic belief to which he had been brought up; here again he made not the slightest effort to play football, and when put on the field reacted with passive resistance; and his unconcealed devotion to philosophy, his resolution to consecrate his life to that, was considered deplorable by his schoolmasters as well as his schoolfellows. Naturally he was appallingly bullied, and the mental scars remained for life. To the end of his days he walked down corridors with a curious shuffle, back to the wall, as if expecting a sudden kick from behind.

Like many such sufferers, McTaggart developed an astonishing loyalty to his school; Clifton College evoked a far deeper loyalty than Trinity College, although the one gave him the life of a free man and a scholar for nearly forty years, while at the other his vocation was slighted and his person continually subject to gross outrage. Clifton demanded extreme devotion from him, not in vain; he was immensely proud to be elected a member of its governing body. In his lifetime he gave philosophical works to the school library, and after his wife's death his entire fortune came to Clifton by his will. So far as I have been able to find out from Cliftonians, his memory has not been kept green there.

The effect on McTaggart's mind and spirit was not so severe as it sometimes is. Lowes Dickinson ascribes to Clifton the fact that McTaggart shed some of the zeal for social reform that some other members of the Ellis clan harboured; but I doubt this. McTaggart's adult political views were not so very different from those of his grandfather's close friend Lord Macaulay; his admiration for Cromwell, his desire to keep Ireland in the United Kingdom, his imperialism about India, his firm patriotism when his country was at war, his desire to see her free from foreign entanglements and secure with a strong Navy, would all I think have been congenial to Macaulay. McTaggart firmly believed in constitutional governments, and hated dictatorships of any political colour. He constantly supported votes for women, and stood up for the equal academic status of women in Cambridge at a time when many of his colleagues held the opposite view. But in any case one of McTaggart's great intellectual virtues was that he chose his opinions *à la carte*, and did not think his choice confined to one or other traditional set meal; people found his combination of certain views inconsistent simply because it did not conform to familiar patterns, but that only showed how illogically many people think.

So McTaggart's mind and attitudes, as they came to be formed, were not really characteristic of the average public-school man; nor were they brutishly Tory, as is sometimes believed – they were much more Whig than Tory. (His philosophical examples constantly take the Whig view of history as an assumed background.) A slightly sinister tune is played in his Hegelian writings about sin and punishment; they read like a rationalization of the prefect-system of his schooldays, in which he had successively been the victim and the wielder of the rod. Using a Hegelian dialectical structure, by which a man progresses from innocence, through a subordinate triad of sin, punishment, and repentance, to a synthesis of achieved virtue, McTaggart explained what the ideal educational system for boys would be: a class division by age, in which older people are in a position of unquestioned moral authority over the younger: arbitrary rules, strictly enforced, which however a young boy with anything in him will now and then break; punishment swift, severe, and humiliating, preferably by a good flogging. He complacently adds that this system has been adopted in English public schools because of the sound national instinct. The best I can say about this effort is that I hope it was produced at least in part *pour épater*: it would certainly shock the solemnly public-spirited British Hegelians whom McTaggart so much disliked and despised.

McTaggart's preoccupation with Hegel seems to have begun at Cambridge. It will have gratified his cheerful, good-humoured, intellectual combativeness; it made him very much an isolated figure, for the British Hegelians and he were very different. He despised their bad logic, their *dirigiste* do-gooder politics, their awed tone of voice about the State as if they spoke of a deity (he himself said a bull or crocodile would be a worthier god); they on their side had no care for the individual person as the bearer of values, or for that love between persons in which McTaggart thought the secret of the Universe lay.

In 1888 McTaggart became an undergraduate at Trinity College, Cambridge, and in 1891 he was elected Fellow. His life was thereafter extremely happy and uneventful. He was a very industrious College and University man; a very patient and clear teacher, and a staunch attender at the necessary business meetings, at which he often gave shrewd advice, constitutional and financial. He greatly enjoyed the convivial side of College life, dined regularly in Hall, and from a gawky youth became very fat, so that he was to be seen pedalling round Cambridge on a custom-built tricycle, being unable to manage a bicycle. (H. G. Wells introduces 'Boggart' into one of his novels, as a man shaped like a bubble, whose thought was all like the blowing of bubbles; Wells's own efforts at philosophizing hardly warrant this assumption of superiority.)

This life was interrupted only by McTaggart's two visits to New Zealand, in 1891 and 1898. His mother, who had connections there, emigrated in 1890 for the sake of his brother's health. He became very fond of New Zealand, and especially enjoyed the absence of the class shibboleths and social divisions that were so irksome in the England of his time. He became fond, too, of a New Zealand girl, Mary Bird, a healthy extrovert who loved riding horses. McTaggart's own horsemanship, as may be imagined, was rather like the White Knight's in Lewis Carroll; but he had the spirit of a paladin in his clumsy body, and he learned to ride after a fashion in order to be with the lady of his heart. He did not win her hand at his first visit, but they corresponded after his return to England, and during a second visit to New Zealand in 1898 they were married. Their married life was one of mutual devotion so long as they both lived. Outsiders found it funny that McTaggart's marriage made so little difference to his outward pattern of life; for example, he continued to dine in Hall most evenings. But the judgement of an outsider in such matters is worthless: their friends knew well that they were devoted lovers.

McTaggart was not a man confined to academic circles. He had many friends in different walks of life, and they found him tolerant (though firm in his own ideas of right and wrong), sympathetic, wise, and ever faithful. He never allowed marriage to break friendships; if a friend got married, he became a friend of them both.

Then came the war of 1914. McTaggart had the straight-forward patriotism of Socrates: too old and fat to fight, he enrolled as a special constable and rode round Cambridge streets on his tricycle trying to detect breaches of the black-out regulations. Many of his contemporaries disgraced their pens by writing foolish pro-war or anti-war literature; McTaggart upheld the dignity of his calling, like his friend Thomas Hardy the poet. To comfort the bereaved he issued a cheap reprint of two chapters from his book *Some Dogmas of Religion*; he wished to show them that philosophy could give rational grounds for hope that death did not separate loving hearts for ever, so that they would not fly to the dubious comforts of revealed religion or of spiritistic superstition.

McTaggart's reputation has suffered because, while he served on the Council of his College during the war, he voted for the dismissal of Bertrand Russell from a College lectureship. Of course the decision is not ascribable to McTaggart alone, and it is curious that he has been singled out for blame. The story is a sorry one; but there were many uglier expressions of national feeling at the time; and by Russell's own account of things in his *Autobiography*, Russell was hardly at that time setting a pattern of wisdom and virtue. Russell must have exasperated McTaggart beyond endurance by talking about nothing except the wickedness of the war; McTaggart was not so tied down in mind to present miseries; the marginal dates in the Trinity MS movingly show that he continued work on the intricate arguments of his *Nature of Existence.*

After the war McTaggart remained convinced that *revanche* by German militarism was to be expected. A muddled man of leftish opinions, as is the habit of such people, invited McTaggart to join in expressing hatred of 'militarism', a protest which will in fact have been directed against the two countries then commonly regarded as dangerously militaristic, France and Poland. McTaggart replied that the Germans had exhausted his limited stock of hatred (and in that loving heart the stock was indeed limited), but that if militarism was to be feared in our century, it was from Germany and possibly from Russia. It cannot be said that history gave the lie to his expectations.

In 1922 McTaggart resigned his College lectureship, though he continued zealously with the unofficial evening lectures he had given for many years for the benefit of non-philosophers. He hoped for leisure to finish his *magnum opus, The Nature of Existence*; but when he was only half way through the revision of his second volume, he fell victim to a painful circulatory disease from which other members of his family had died. In face of death he was strikingly serene; he died on 18 January 1925. By his own wish, the memorial tablet in the antechapel of Trinity College bears a Latin text from Spinoza saying: 'The free man thinks of nothing less than he does of death, and his wisdom is a meditation not of death but of life.'

McTaggart's work

In this book I aim at giving a handy guide to McTaggart's metaphysical thought by sketching the main lines of argument boldly and clearly, with a minimum of adverse criticism; I intend it of course as a stimulus and a preparation for careful reading of McTaggart's own works, not as a substitute for that. I begin by stating what the work was all in aid of. Nobody could properly judge the architecture of a building if he simply did not know whether it was designed for a monastery, a public school, a store-house, or a prison. And though individual bits of argument in McTaggart have an independent interest, as we shall see, nobody can really get to grips with his system without feeling at least some imaginative sympathy for its principal aims.

In McTaggart we find a curious union of mysticism and rationalism. From time to time he had mystical experiences that gave him an utterly satisfying and unshakable conviction that he had penetrated through appearances and divined the secret of the Universe. That secret was, in a word, love; and what McTaggart meant by that much-abused and grossly ambiguous word was the actual devotion of one person to another – David's love for Jonathan or Robert Browning's love for his Elizabeth. This mystical vision convinced him, but he realized that it would be neither convincing nor evidential for others.

To get his vision over to others, he used the way of discursive argument. He had had a sight of the answer at the back of the book; if he worked the sum right, his working must come up with the same answer. The continued intellectual effort of his life was to find rational arguments that would prove the world to be nothing but persons loving one another. If one argument was demolished (and he subjected all his arguments to rigorous test, both by self-criticism and by getting friends to read his MS), then he would not be discouraged but would start again. The labour that went into his few books was very great; he wrote five complete drafts of everything he published. His revision of the second volume of *The Nature of Existence* was only half-finished at the time of his death (he had completed Drafts A and B and half-written Draft C); but he appears to have been satisfied this time that in essentials his life's task was accomplished; the Trinity MS bears a pencil inscription on its last page, addressed to McTaggart's wife: 'Heart of my heart, have I done well?'

McTaggart did not conceive philosophy as something just for professional philosophers. Upon the metaphysical dogmas a man accepts there will turn his whole attitude to the Universe; he can indeed avoid having any such attitudes by living for bodily needs like a beast or by blinkered attention to some limited human concern, e.g. a political party, but so to live is unworthy of a man. Metaphysics, he thought, suffered from neglect because people either did not realize how serious its questions were, or thought some traditional or revealed religion had given the essential answers. In the first chapter of this book we shall see why McTaggart was sceptical of the claims made by religious believers; for him human reason was the key to a solution that would become generally satisfactory if only enough good minds took up metaphysics. He earnestly strove to spread a serious interest in metaphysics among men who were not professional philosophers: his evening lectures, deservedly popular, and his very simply written book *Some Dogmas of Religion*, are sufficient testimony to this.

Educated in a conscientiously unbelieving Victorian family, McTaggart started with no inclination to take Christianity seriously; and the variety of Christianity that he encountered at his public school is not likely to have appeared either emotionally congenial, or in the smallest degree intellectually or morally respectable. He constantly assumed that the God of Christian belief would be 'personal' in the sense of being one single person; he never encountered, so far as I can discover, the doctrine that the eternal life of God is the mutual love of three Persons, for he never considers the relation of this doctrine to his own view of eternal life. He argued in any event that all forms of theism must be rejected in view of the thesis that time is unreal; a thesis which, however paradoxical, he regarded as admitting of absolute demonstration, quite apart from the exigences of his own system. It is not really surprising that the figure of Christ given in the Gospels did not excite McTaggart's admiration. The God-centred Dominical teaching would appear to him as the opinionated propagation of doctrines that are demonstrably false.

For the rational establishment of his own metaphysical insights McTaggart at first looked to the logic of Hegel in the *Greater Logic* and the *Encyclopaedia*: the task of philosophy must be to arrange the fundamental categories of ontology in an order of thesis, antithesis, and synthesis, culminating in an 'absolute idea', a completely adequate category in which all the inadequacies and imbalances of lower categories are harmoniously resolved. This 'absolute idea' is conceived abstractly, but it serves as a criterion for judging the concrete appearances of things in everyday experience: all elements of everyday experience that do not measure up to the requirements of the 'absolute idea' must be regarded as more or less delusive. Already in this Hegelian period McTaggart was sure that only one concrete representation of the Universe could meet the requirements: the Universe is a society of perfect persons who perfectly and eternally know and love each other. In all the multifarious delusion that is our everyday life, love is the one element that is certainly not delusion, whatever cynical worldlings may think.

I know too little about Hegel to comment on McTaggart's Hegelian writings. His acquaintance with Hegel's writings was like the chapter-and-verse knowledge of the Bible that out-of-the-way Protestant sectarians often have; the unanimous judgement of Hegelian experts appears to be that McTaggart's interpretations of Hegel were as perverse as these sectarians' interpretations of the Bible. Even in his most Hegelian days McTaggart rejected many of Hegel's writings as, so to speak, deutero-canonical. It was just in these that the contemporary British Hegelians had most pleasure; they delighted in Hegel's views on politics and society, and had little knowledge of Hegel's logic; between them and McTaggart there was hardly any meeting of minds.

McTaggart wrote Hegel out of his system by producing an elaborate detailed commentary on Hegel's logic. Though he still expresses a conviction in principle that the dialectic method is the right way to set about metaphysical thought, he found many broken links in Hegel's chain of reasoning.

Thenceforth McTaggart resorted to a different philosophical method, reminiscent of Descartes, Spinoza, and Leibniz. He still held that the right beginning for metaphysics was the construction of an abstract ontology dealing with the bloodless categories of reality, existence, substance and characteristics, whole and part, etc., and that information empirically given must be rejected as delusive if it fails to conform to the abstract scheme. But he no longer thought the abstract ontology required a new dialectical method: ordinary logic, reinvigorated as it had been by the thought of his great Cambridge contemporaries, would be entirely adequate to the task. The starting point would be a clear and distinct understanding of the indefinable ideas involved, and of the indemonstrable principles, self-evident if only confusion and prejudice were removed, that linked these indefinables synthetically together. Kantian inquiries about how we can have synthetic *a priori* knowledge were far from McTaggart's way of thinking: he was not the man to worry about how we know that we know.

By means of his abstract ontology McTaggart set about judging the appearances: he quickly concluded that both time and matter were illusory; even more paradoxically (though less so in the age of Freud than at a time when philosophers commonly held self-consciousness to be inerrant) he unsparingly rejected as delusive most of our introspective judgements about our mental life. He convinced himself that the only description of reality that could without contradiction satisfy his *a priori* requirements was a description of a society of persons transparent to one another's loving contemplation. Though built up out of materials supplied by present experience, this description seems to be refuted by present experience. McTaggart would reply, like Sherlock Holmes, that when everything that is impossible has been excluded, whatever remains, however improbable it may seem, must be true.

McTaggart recognized, however, that the fact of misperception, of the vast illusion which on his view is concealing from us the nature of the Universe, must itself be fully and fairly described, explained so far as possible, and at the least shown not to be logically incompatible with his main doctrines. A great deal of the second volume of *The Nature of Existence* is devoted to this desperate task. As a result of these Herculean labours, McTaggart thought he had done far more than to rebut a seemingly inescapable refutation: he had also gained a positive insight into that real structure which we misperceive as series of events in time, and could conclude from this that what philosophy reveals as an eternal blessed state of love is *sub specie temporis* future for all of us. But he altogether rejected all forms of cheap and easy optimism: the enormous good of the final consummation does not exclude extreme and prolonged evil in this scene of our sorrow, and this we must simply face.

In McTaggart there was no painful division between head and heart, philosophy and life. His philosophy of love accorded with a life that was filled with love: the life of a good son, a loving husband, a constant and understanding friend of many people in different walks of life. He had expressed a resolve that neither the pains of life nor the pains of death should make him flee to irrational comforts or abandon beliefs that his reason told him were solidly grounded; his resolve did not fail in the dark days of war or in the pains of his last illness.

1 Metaphysical dogmas

The two works of McTaggart that I shall be considering in this outline are *Some Dogmas of Religion* and *The Nature of Existence*.[1] *Some Dogmas of Religion* is a work addressed to the general educated public, not just to professional philosophers; it is a great pity that at present it is available only in an expensive reprint. The contents of the book are as follows:

1 A popular account of McTaggart's doctrines concerning human immortality and pre-existence. These two chapters formed the small separately printed work that McTaggart issued during the First World War.

2 Three chapters (and a conclusion) containing McTaggart's attack on theism.

3 A chapter on free will: this states determinism clearly, but to my mind adds little to what other determinists have said.

4 Two chapters on the nature of dogma or metaphysical belief.

In the book itself these contents come in the order 4, 1, 3, 2. I shall be discussing 1 and 2 in the last chapter of the present book, and the reader will find they throw light on the more formally presented reasoning of *The Nature of Existence* on the same topics; 2 also contains important and original reflection on the hoary old topic of evil and omnipotence. I see no need to discuss 3 in this book.

The present chapter is concerned with the topic of 4. My own debt to McTaggart in my thought on the topic is very great, and on these issues of philosophical method and aims I largely agree

---

[1] I give references to both books by section numbers; numbers without prefix are from *The Nature of Existence* and run consecutively through the two volumes of this work, vol. 1 ending at 293; references to *Some Dogmas of Religion* are prefaced with *DR*.

with him. So in this chapter I am speaking much more *in propria persona* than I shall be in subsequent chapters.

McTaggart begins by talking about metaphysics and about dogmas, that is metaphysical propositions. A metaphysical concern is part of the human condition; not a disease artificially generated in philosophy departments in order that it may then be cured by linguistic analysis, using one or other fashionable therapy. In a Leeds public house I heard two elderly working men arguing for a whole hour about whether tomorrow comes. The dispute became a bit repetitious after a time, but the initial arguments *pro* and *contra* were of great interest.

Of course tomorrow will come. Tomorrow is May 18th isn't it? Well, May 18th will come; so tomorrow will come.

No, that can't be right. If something is going to come, some time it'll be right to say it has come. But it will never be right to say tomorrow *has* come. So tomorrow never will come.

It comes naturally to men to pose such problems; but a very little thought shows that the untying of this knot about tomorrow, and of others like it, will require techniques, e.g. of formal logic, that cannot be quickly acquired. And here we come on to what McTaggart calls metaphysics – 'the *systematic* study of the *ultimate* nature of reality' (*DR* 1).

I have italicized two words in McTaggart's definition. 'Ultimate' has rather unhappy associations – with the woolly idealists, whom McTaggart so much despised, who spoke of how things are 'in the end', as if this were somehow different from the way things are. McTaggart's meaning can be quite plainly set forth. Things are not always what they seem: that is so far mere common sense. Some philosophers, notably Protagoras and Bertrand Russell, have tried to reject the distinction between the way we perceive things to be and the way things are; but we could not avoid either paradox or intellectual labour if we tried to take this rejection seriously. If however we accept the distinction, we are left with the question: What are the principles on which we decide what is real and what is only illusory appearance? A systematic account of these principles will by definition be metaphysical.

McTaggart, like the young Wittgenstein, insists that his problems are not abstract but supremely concrete, not impractical but supremely important. For example, the appearance of things is that when a man dies that is the end of him; yet hardly any belief is commoner in mankind than the belief that *this* appearance is delusive – that when a man has died there is a possibility, or even a certainty, that he or some part of him will survive death. It is irrelevant that carelessness and inattention are a good way of putting the subject out of our minds; that no more affects the truth of the matter, or its importance, than the way cigarette smokers can put lung cancer out of their minds.

All the same, very few men have undertaken that systematic study of such questions which constitutes metaphysics: and the agreed results reached from so many centuries of intense intellectual labour are not very impressive. Why not then renounce metaphysics in favour of billiards and backgammon? Well, there are those, like McTaggart, who will seek because they must. And in his courses for non-philosophers McTaggart must have given many people something of his own eagerness to know.

Whereas metaphysicians, using discursive reason, have achieved so little in the way of assured truth, there are various religions that claim to give man certain and relatively comprehensive answers to many of his searching questions. The belief in the truth of metaphysical dogmas thus forms part of many people's religion; McTaggart holds it is an essential part. A religion, he thinks, can no more live without dogmas than a man without bones. Remove the dogmas and the whole collapses to a shapeless jelly of emotion.

It would in fact be very difficult to say in advance concerning any kind of metaphysical dogma that it would not be relevant to a man's religion – or even, that it would not be directly relevant. McTaggart's attempt to give an example of a clearly irrelevant dogma was not a success. He could not see that believing or disbelieving in the existence of matter need affect a man's religion. But Berkeley was embarrassed by the conflict of his immaterialism with a Christian dogma: the dogma that (by God's creation) the material world, sun, moon, and stars, land

and sea, existed before there were any men or other animals to perceive all these things. (Of course modern science gives us no reason to doubt this dogma.) And on the other hand Berkeley was delighted by the fact that his immaterialism excludes the dogma of Transubstantiation; this makes quite a difference to a man's religion, as a Protestant Bishop in Ireland engaged in controversy with Papists could not help knowing. Someone who denies the dogma cannot well remain a *bona fide* Catholic; he certainly cannot if he denies it on Berkeley's grounds.

Already in McTaggart's time there were those who disagreed about dogma's being essential to religion; following Matthew Arnold, they held that some sort of enthusiasm for virtue, or for a way of life, is the essential thing in religion, and that dogmas can be cheerfully dropped. A view found in some philosophy departments nowadays (but hardly popular outside academic circles) has to my mind a strong family likeness to this way of thinking. The favoured language is of course now quite different, but I do not think that here the medium is the message. I once heard a lecture in which we were sententiously told that if we have the right standards of what constitutes harm, nothing can harm the good man; this, one gathered, is the important thing for religion – such matters as the Providence of God and the survival of death are not religious concerns.

I can only say that McTaggart's attack on this sort of thing seems to me to hit the bull's eye. A virtue that is indifferent to its own ill-success in its endeavours is hardly consistent; a virtue so extreme as to be indifferent to other men's misery has passed into its opposite (*D R* 19). But if one cares about the success of one's endeavours in relieving human misery, then an enthusiasm for virtue brings not peace but a sword. Peace can come only with a dogma that guarantees eventual victory for the good. And I agree with McTaggart that by clinging to the word 'religion' for this dogma-free enthusiasm men are only kidding themselves that they still have what in fact they have lost.

I will add one further consideration to McTaggart's: there is no coherent, let alone tolerable, view of harm that would make it true that the good man can come to no harm. For man's will is labile, and a good man may turn to the bad; and it may seem to be a matter of accidents beyond his control whether his losing his wits or his health, or encountering some insupportable temptation, does not destroy his hard-won virtue. It is otherwise if one believes in the Providence and Grace of God; one may then believe that God does not allow those who do not willingly desert him to be led into wickedness by force of circumstance, and that the faithful servant gets enough grace to persevere in goodness from day to day. (Some Christians have even believed that experiencing some crisis of conversion, or again keeping the Nine First Fridays, can guarantee in advance that one will in fact persevere to the end.) But of course this is a matter of dogma; and whereas dogmatic sorts of Christianity offer such a guarantee, obviously the new undogmatic Christianity can offer only a wholly inadequate *Ersatz*, stones for bread.

It would obviously be very agreeable if certainty about dogmatic questions could be attained without the arduous labours of the metaphysician: and McTaggart next considers various proposed ways of achieving such certainty. I shall cover the same ground here as McTaggart does in the second chapter of his book, but the order in which I shall take up points is slightly different from his.

1   *DR* 32–7: If a man is directly convinced, apart from any authority or revelation, that some dogma is true, ought he to hold on to this conviction and let himself off examining the matter further? And if *A* has such a conviction, can this be a good reason for *B* to accept the truth of the dogma?

2   *DR* 38–40: Is any dogma to be held worthy of acceptance on the ground that it already is held by everybody who counts?

3   *DR* 44–52: Can any dogma be excluded from credibility on the ground that the world would be really too dreadful if the dogma were true, or would become intolerable if the dogma came to be widely believed?

4   *DR* 41–3: Can we justifiably accept a dogma on someone's authority or testimony?

5   *DR* 53–4: Can a dogma be commended to us on the score

that our minds are too weak and ignorant for us to be in a position to reject it?

6   *DR* 55–8: Can we replace the idea of believing a dogma with the idea of loving trust in a person?

1   We are here considering the case of firm unreasoned conviction, not of mystical experience: for example, not the man who says he has seen God, but the man who says it is obvious that there is a God, the matter needs no proof. About this case I have hardly anything of my own to say; I think McTaggart's remarks and arguments are almost entirely correct.

First, a man may be mistaken when he claims to have an immediate certainty that a proposition is true. He may be confusing two propositions together, and when the difference between them is made plain to him he may change his testimony about what is immediately certain to him. Or again, he may think his certainty is immediate when it is in fact based upon reasons; and when these reasons have been brought into the open he may abandon the proposition he was certain of, because the reasons strike him as bad ones.

Again, a belief that is not based upon reasons may be based on prejudices early acquired, and when this becomes clear to the believer it may shake his belief. A man has no right to claim an immediate certainty that cannot be subject to these sorts of tests. And if even after such tests he is disposed to persist in his claim, the only point of his making the claim to others is to explain why they should not try to shake his belief by argument. It is mere arrogance for *A* to say to *B*: 'I am quite convinced of this, so you ought to be convinced of it too!' If *A* merely believes, and can give no grounds for his belief, that is an exceedingly weak ground for *B* to believe the like. We can indeed get nowhere except on the basis of *some* unquestioned certainties; but these need not be certainties about religious dogmas, they may be about matters where agreement is happily easier to secure.

2   Why should people who dissent from it *not* count, when we are trying to show that everybody who counts assents to a certain religious dogma? It has sometimes been said that no-

body can in good faith deny certain dogmas: St Paul in particular appears to say this about the existence of God. McTaggart is very sceptical as to whether in fact there is *any* religious dogma that is 'certain to all men, except to those who have disqualified themselves by a life of exceptional wickedness' (*DR* 39); but of course St Paul or St Augustine could reply that because of the Fall wickedness and bad faith are not the exception but the rule. However, this sort of reply already assumes a lot of dogmas; I do not think anybody would hold just on the basis of observing his fellow-men, and not on the basis of dogmas already accepted, that dissent from a particular dogma must be due to bad faith. So the position is this: one dogma, say the existence of God, can claim a favourable opinion poll if the right voters only are counted; but the disqualification of the other voters will need to be justified by another dogma or dogmas, which may even presuppose the dogma we first thought of. The prospect, then, of establishing a dogma by general consent cannot be called bright.

3   I agree with McTaggart in finding appeals of the form 'You cannot believe this, it would be too dreadful' to be intellectually and morally squalid; I may remark that no such appeal is to be found in the Old or New Testament. Some Christian apologists have resorted to such appeals in blithe unawareness of how easily the like appeal could be made against what they themselves believe. We are told that it would be too dreadful to believe that a man once dead is done for, or to believe that there is no God who will see justice done to the needy and oppressed; but then we may find that the very man who makes this appeal himself believes that the entire human race is involved in the terrible calamity of Original Sin, and that many men incur the even greater calamity of everlasting damnation.

4   The next set of topics is the one on which McTaggart's discussion is to my mind far less satisfactory. He raises the questions whether a set of dogmas can justifiably be accepted on the word of an authority, and whether the authority can give itself credit by miracles, in particular by the miracle of prophesying

the future. Miracles are far too difficult a topic for me to do more than mention it now. I shall confine myself to some general remarks on the intellectual ethics of accepting testimony and authority. On this topic I am afraid McTaggart has little in the way of light and leading to give us; for he appears to have uncritically accepted the common view that reliance upon testimony and authority is a matter of confirming a theory inductively (see *D R* 34, 35).

I have little positive to say about this; but it seems to me that inductivism gives a totally wrong account of the matter. However much weight we give to induction in our theory of knowledge (and notoriously some modern philosophers of science hold a very depreciative view of induction) it is obvious that the inductive conclusions anyone could justifiably reach on the basis of his own experience alone would be exceedingly meagre; and it is surely fantastic to suppose that these conclusions from personal experience could embrace a corpus of inductive knowledge about human veracity and reliability sufficient to justify the extent to which we do in fact rely upon testimony and authority.

The obvious truth of what I have just said is disguised from people who read an inductivist writer like Hume by his slippery use of the term 'experience'; he plays fast and loose, using it to mean now the individual's experience and now the experience of mankind. Possibly Hume's own experience would establish the relation between a creaking noise and the opening of his chamber door; but when he claims that his own experience tells him what happens to a letter in between its being posted and his receiving it, one can only gape at the enormity of the falsehood. When talking about other topics, miracles let us say, he unblushingly uses 'experience' to mean human experience generally; he assumes that there is a known corpus of human experience, and does not ask how this corpus becomes available to any one of us. But clearly it is only in virtue of testimony and authority that a sufficient corpus of experience can be got together to be a foundation for the sort of inductions that we do rely upon, whether about human nature or about other things. There would be a fatal vicious circle if trust in testimony and authority had to rest upon inductions about the circumstances in which men will both learn the truth and tell it; for such inductions would themselves be miserably ill-founded if they did not rest upon a body of information which can itself have been got together only by reliance upon testimony and authority.

Witnesses and authorities contradict one another, so it is logically impossible to trust them all. There are occasions where we should judge the unanimous testimony of eye-witnesses to have been mistaken, and the unanimous view of the accepted authorities in one generation has been rejected by their successors. For the moment I can say little about the criteria to be applied.

Among authorities who disagree are of course those authorities who claim to teach us the truth about God. At this point, as McTaggart remarks, the dogma that God can neither deceive nor be deceived is of key importance (*DR* 43). A corpus of traditional belief may include stories about the Gods' deceiving and being deceived: the Greek religious tradition is one example. It would of course be very nasty to have to believe that we were ruled by such Gods; fortunately, we can reject any revelation that purports to tell us about such Gods, not out of wishful thinking, but with a good logical conscience; someone who claimed to speak in the name of such Gods would be condemned out of his own mouth as a man whom we need not consider a witness of truth. Whether or not the key dogma of God's telling the truth is accepted, no alleged revelation inconsistent with this dogma deserves a moment's notice.

Again, people have seriously doubted whether *any* kind of action is always wrong, and must therefore doubt whether in particular it is always wrong to lie about the truths of religion. But that such lying is always forbidden by God must be part of the content of a revelation that we are meant to take seriously; or at least, it must not be part of the revelation that some religious lies are pious, or even, that they may be venial; otherwise the revelation once more destroys its own credibility by destroying the credit of its messengers. And in fact it is part of the traditional Christian teaching that a witness to Christian truth must absolutely never lie when he is delivering his message, whatever the cost to himself or to his nearest and dearest. This does not

B

of course prove that Christian tradition to be God's truth; it merely satisfies a condition *sine qua non*, without which Christianity would simply not be intellectually respectable.

A further condition *sine qua non* is that a revelation must be consistent if it is to be credible. I do not say that a revelation must be provably consistent; by now, the information really ought to have got around from formal logicians to the learned world in general that the credibility of a system does not depend on our having a proof of its consistency, and that demand for such a proof may be unreasonable. Aquinas purports to offer proofs that certain questions about God are undecidable: the true answer, whatever it may be, can neither be proved nor disproved, so that if we are to have the truth God must reveal it for our belief. Proving that no proof can settle certain questions may once have seemed and may still seem a paradoxical idea; it ought not now to appear absurd.

What can be required for a revelation's credibility is that it should not be provably inconsistent; and it will certainly be that if the story authoritatively told changes from one generation to another. The truth about God cannot itself change; and if a professed witness of the truth changes his story, then one time or the other he must have been demanding assent when such a demand was mere impudence. As Thomas Hobbes might have said: Popes succeed one another; and one bishop passeth, another cometh; nay, Heaven and Earth shall pass; but not one tittle of the Law of Contradiction shall pass; for it is the Eternal Law of God.

My last point under this head is that a credible authority must go back to an original revealer who claimed not to believe but to know: say, to Moses who saw God face to face, or to Jesus who spoke with authority and not as the scribes. In human affairs, one man may believe something happened because another man told him, and there may be many such links; but if there is no reason to think the chain ends in an eye-witness, then the whole chain falls to the ground. Similarly here. Latterly I have heard people speak of the *faith* that Jesus had in his Father and his own mission. If this language (of course quite untraditional) is taken at its face value, then Jesus did not *know* who he was and why he was in the world – he just had strong convictions about the matter. But, as McTaggart has said, *A*'s firm conviction that something is true about God is no reason at all why *B* should believe it; not even if *A* is a highly impressive person – for of course one highly impressive person has held beliefs inconsistent with those of another such person, and we cannot then follow them both. If Jesus only *believed*, the whole chain of belief that ends in his words falls to the ground. A long line of blind men, each trustfully holding to the one just in front, may all keep to the road so long as there is one sighted man in front; but if the blind lead the blind – ! If Jesus Christ was blind and ignorant as we are, then faith in him is vain.

5 McTaggart next considers the sort of people who urge us to accept dogmas simply and solely because we are in complete conceptual confusion about the terms in which the dogmas are stated. Unfortunately he is quite correct in his representation of the matter. The dogmas of the Trinity and the Incarnation are stated by using the term 'person' and 'nature': there have been apologists who think it enough ground for commending these dogmas to our acceptance if they can make out that we really have extremely confused ideas about human personality and human nature, so that we cannot rely on any principles that might exclude dogmas about Divine Persons and the Divine Nature. Similarly, our not having the least idea what the substance of bread is, or even what phrases of the form 'the substance of so-and-so' mean, has been offered as a ground for the unhesitating acceptance of ecclesiastical teaching that one of these unintelligible entities sometimes takes the place of another. McTaggart protests, to my mind rightly, that if we are muddled in our use of terms, we ought not to fancy that blind acceptance of one unintelligible dogma rather than another stated in these terms will do us any good: let us rather try to clear up the muddle.

Even McTaggart's unkind caricature, that people might as well be urged, on the ground of their weakness and ignorance, to believe that the Law of Diminishing Returns devours purple quadratic equations (*DR* 54), is not too gross in view of some apologetic argument. Theologians have maintained that the Persons of the Trinity are subsistent relations. This is not a formula in a creed or a decree of a Church Council, but a piece of speculative theology; and it certainly calls for explanation – how can a person *be* a relation? Now I once heard this thesis defended, not by any attempt to explain it, but by an argument that we can hardly expect to know what we are talking about when we are concerned with relations; relations are anyhow very peculiar entities; and if some of the relations that actually obtain are not even real, why could not other relations that actually obtain have enough reality to *be* persons? Only McTaggart's satire is an adequate comment on this defence.

It does not follow that no idea of mysteries' being worthy of belief is defensible; and the defence I shall sketch is well rooted in Christian tradition. A mystery of faith is not supposed to be blankly unintelligible: even the simplest believer can gain some positive understanding and give real assent to what he understands, and even the wisest theologian cannot attain to full comprehension. The obedience of faith is needed for the first understanding – *credo ut intelligam* – but this venture is rewarded by ever deeper understanding. Apparent contradictions will crop up, but there can be no genuine conflict either internal or external, either within the sphere of dogmas accepted by faith or with truth otherwise known. As Aquinas taught, truth cannot contradict truth; and any alleged disproofs of a dogma of faith will be *rationes solubiles*, refutable, if we can only see the way, by the impartial standards of ordinary logic. We cannot indeed hope for a once-for-all consistency proof, but in the light of modern logic we know that the supplying of a consistency proof is often an unreasonable demand even in non-theological contexts. And faith is progressively strengthened and confirmed both by the failure of attempted refutations, and by the way that concepts refined in theological controversy (e.g. those of personality and intensive magnitude) increase our understanding of the world we live in – just as the sun, too bright to gaze upon directly, lights up all the objects around us.

6   I shall now deal with the argument that we should get away

from the business of assent to dogmatic propositions, and think rather in terms of loving trust in a Person. I shall discuss this differently from McTaggart, because I think the best way to discuss it involves notions of intentionality that have become prominent in recent philosophy but were hardly over the horizon when McTaggart was writing.

Love of God or of Jesus Christ is quite different from love of a person we are acquainted with in the ordinary way. 'No man has seen God at any time'; apart from alleged visions, which I cannot now discuss, no living man has seen Jesus Christ either. In this life we know God and Jesus Christ not by acaquintance but by description. No doubt this does not exclude genuine love and trust; an old Cavalier may have loved and trusted King Charles I although he had only heard of him and had never met him. But we cannot properly leave out of account the adequacy of the description under which the loved person is thought of. As I have written elsewhere, a man's love for a woman, no matter how great the significance for his emotional life, cannot be held to latch on to *her* if she is for him a *princesse lointaine* about whose actual attributes he has the most fantastic misconceptions. Now the like possibilities cannot be excluded in regard to God and Jesus Christ; for men's conceptions of God and Christ are extremely various, as a very slight examination will prove:

> The vision of Christ which thou dost see
> Is my vision's greatest enemy.

A *sufficient* degree of misconception will prevent the love a man feels from latching on to its alleged object at all; what he loves will be a mere imaginary phantasm, called by a familiar name. It is not for me to judge when this happens; but the variety of men's conceptions means it is not open to serious doubt that such misdirection of love does sometimes happen. But then the importance of dogma once more becomes apparent; only by believing true dogmas about God and Christ can a man be secured against such a fatally delusive love. It was a rational teaching of the medieval theologians that faith cannot be *founded* on love, that on the contrary, supernatural love of God and Christ presupposes a faith exercised in assent to those propositions which are called the articles of faith.

McTaggart ends his discussion with the remark that, whatever may be the dogmas we are intellectually justified in accepting, we shall be amazingly lucky if we do not need a kind of courage and faith to hang on to them. The changes and chances of this mortal life may well make a dogma we have accepted seem too good or too bad to be true. McTaggart is of course right; I may add that the same body of dogmas may seem now unbelievably cheerful and now unbelievably gloomy. The consolations of religion may sound hollow over a child's grave; the death of a beloved friend may make it an intolerable thought that he died in great danger of hell. But whatever the truth of these matters may be, it cannot change with these incidents and with the resulting fluctuations in our feelings.

We find Boswell ludicrous for being afraid of judgement and damnation at night when he was feverish and in pain, but having a more cheerful view of his Creator's mercy in the morning when he felt better. But a man who talks solemnly of the need for an agonizing reappraisal of revealed religion in a world that has seen the massacres of Oświęcim and Hiroshima is not a bit more intellectually respectable than poor Boswell. Such talk may be solemn, but it is not serious. The Thirty Years War is none the less a fact for being temporally remote from us, and it was fought allegedly for the cause of Christian truth. If the occurrence of the Thirty Years War does not already refute the Christian religion, then the massacres that seem to be specially frequent in what I once heard a lady on the radio call 'this Age of Kindness' cannot refute it either; and if the occurrence of that war did already refute Christianity, then equally the later horrors are a superfluous consideration.

I see no reason to be indulgent to people who deprave our standards of discussion by giving vent to such bellyaching 're-appraisals' in cold blood. For people whose beliefs are irrationally shaken by the shock of a personal misfortune, one can only feel compassion: there but for the Grace of God – ! One can only pray that such shocks may not lead the sufferer to forsake the Truth; and each of us has to bear in mind for his own hour of death the prayer whose spirit McTaggart commended, atheist as he was:

Thou most worthy Judge Eternal, suffer us not at our last hour for any pains of death to fall from thee.

2 Reality and existence

McTaggart begins his metaphysical inquiry in *The Nature of Existence* by stating that *prima facie* the existent and the real are related as species and genus. He explains reality by the dictum 'Whatever is, is real'; but at the same time he thinks predications of unreality are sometimes correct, e.g. if the subject is 'the Duke of London in 1919' or 'the fourth angle of a triangle'. We cannot make sense of this if we stick to McTaggart's way of speaking and treat reality as a *quality* of things; but from what he writes elsewhere it is clear that this way of speaking is not to be taken seriously. Much later in the book he makes it plain that he agrees with Bertrand Russell in holding that 'X is unreal' is true just when 'X' is read as a description that describes nothing (629).

McTaggart absolutely rejected any idea of relativizing reality or ascribing degrees to it. He rejected the talk of Mrs Gamp as real in a novel of Dickens or somebody's dream-world but not in the everyday world; it is the novel or the dream that is real, *simpliciter*, not Mrs Gamp (3). Similarly, there cannot be degrees of reality, degrees of *there being* a so-and-so; a pain in my leg, say, may be more or less vehement, but there can be no question of degree about *whether there is* a pain in my leg. Nor can there be degrees of approximation to reality any more than there can be degrees of its intensity. Anything that there is, there just is: a thing cannot *nearly* be without *quite* being (4).

On these matters McTaggart is plainly right; and since this hydra of error, only scotched and not killed by Russell, seems now to be reviving, this good sense is needed in our day. A peculiar twist of error in recent writing is to speak of fictional people and dead people as if there were no logical change of key. There is nothing logically peculiar about the proper names of dead people. It belongs to the ordinary use of a man's name that people should speak of him in his absence; if he happens to die, without the speakers' knowledge, between one conversation about him and another, his death does not alter the logical status of what is said, by some sort of logical action at a distance. But when what is grammatically a proper noun is used by a novelist who *makes believe* this is somebody's name, the noun in this use does not, and was never intended to, name anybody. A philosopher who assimilates our use of 'Adolf Hitler' and Dickens's use of 'Mrs Gamp' is just deceiving himself and his readers.

Again, some Idealists were apparently willing to say that time or evil (say) is real as an appearance, or 'phenomenally' real, but not *really*, 'ultimately', real. Ayer has implied that McTaggart talked this way,[1] but this is quite untrue. On the contrary, McTaggart expressly deprecates such language. He did indeed draw the distinction between appearance and reality in a very unusual way; but his way of expressing himself would not be 'Tables are phenomenally real but not ultimately real' but rather 'There are no tables in reality, there are only real things that are misperceived as tables' (520).

In writings on the philosophy of religion people often want to say that 'time is real from the human point of view but not from God's point of view'. For McTaggart this is a shameful equivocation, a dodging of the issue whether temporal succession is real or illusory. In the present context God is being assumed to be omniscient, so the way God sees things to be is just the way they are; if then God does not see the world as temporal and changing, time and change are not 'real from the human point of view', but merely systematic false appearances; to us there appear to be time and change, but we are deluded.

McTaggart uses several times over a style of argument designed to show that it is self-contradictory to say 'There is only an appearance of X but not any real X'; *sometimes* even a false appearance of an X implies there being some real X in the world. For example, no philosophical argument can charm away pain from the Universe: if there is an illusory appearance of pain,

[1] A. J. Ayer, *Metaphysics and Common Sense* (Macmillan, 1967), pp. 65ff.

then there is real pain, because such an illusion is an *unpleasant* illusion (857). Nor could we consistently be extreme pessimists and say that there is no pleasure in the world, that the appearance of pleasure is e.g. an illusion produced by temporary remissions of pain. If you seem to be enjoying something, you must really be enjoying your experience, however much of a fool's paradise you are living in (858). And if only a person can have illusions, it cannot be an illusion that some person exists. By this characteristic turn of argument McTaggart draws a limit to scepticism.

We may now turn to McTaggart's understanding of existence. Existence, he holds, cannot be defined; we can get over the meaning of the term by saying which things are existent. What are in the first place existent are concrete individuals, or as McTaggart says substances. If time is real, events that happen to substances are existent. Characteristics, i.e. qualities and relations, of existent things are themselves existent; and so are facts about existent things, whether the things are substances, events, characteristics, or facts. (We shall return to facts later.)

McTaggart thus uses the term 'existent' pretty much as Frege uses the term '*wirklich*', 'actual'; and I shall sometimes use 'actual' as a variant on 'existent', which I think often makes McTaggart's meaning clearer.

Is there anything non-actual? McTaggart considers various candidates for recognition as non-actual objects. (1) '*Proposition*' is the term used by many philosophers for that which is thought or believed or asserted, as opposed to the thinking oɪ believing or asserting that is done by a given person. I use a capital letter for 'Proposition' in this special sense, to distinguish it from the more traditional use of 'proposition' to mean a bit of language with a certain kind of use. (2) Various philosophers have ascribed to *characteristics* a reality independent of the things characterized: thus scholastics considered whether there are *universalia ante res*, universals prior in nature to the things that instantiate them. (3) Again, many philosophers have thought there are *possibilities* that are real independently of their actualization.

For various reasons, McTaggart disqualifies all of these

claimants. In order to understand how he disqualified them, we need first to discuss a class of actualities that play a great part in McTaggart's philosophy: the class of *facts*. To specify a particular fact, we use a *that*-clause: 'the fact', say, 'that this table is oblong'. An equivalent form of words would be 'the oblong shape of this table'. If this table is not oblong but square or oval, then either form of words is a vacuous designation to which no fact answers. Only true assertions or suppositions or beliefs have facts corresponding to them; their truth consists in a correspondence-relation to a fact.

This doctrine of facts was very much of a common Cambridge teaching in McTaggart's day. The young Wittgenstein, during his stay in Cambridge before the First World War, was solidly persuaded of this ontology of facts, and we find it playing a conspicuous role in his *Tractatus*. A classical and very clear exposition is to be found in John Wisdom's *Problems of Mind and Matter* (Cambridge University Press, 1963).

A common Cambridge opinion about facts was that a fact has *parts* corresponding to the syntactical parts of the relevant sentence: if the bag actually is on the table, then the fact that things are so has as parts: the bag, the relation *on*, and the table. (In the Cambridge jargon the word 'constituent' or 'component' was used instead of 'part', but that makes no odds.) Now if we think of the fact as a sort of union of these three components, it might make us wonder whether the relation *on* has a different sort of reality from the bag and the table, and whether it could 'subsist' (as people used to say) independently of any actual objects' lying on one another. McTaggart, as I said, rejected the idea of *universalia ante res*; he rejected also this view of facts' being made up of parts. Though there would be something common to the bag's being on the table and Alexander's being on Bucephalus, the characteristic *on* would have no being except in facts.

I think the best way to expound McTaggart's doctrine and make it plausible is to borrow a notion from Frege (with whose works I believe McTaggart was not acquainted). We may think of a certain *function* that takes bodies as arguments and facts about bodies as values; if we represent this function by the letter

'ϕ', then the bag's being on the table will be ϕ(the bag, the table), and Alexander's being on Bucephalus will be ϕ(Alexander, Bucephalus), and so on. Being values of the same function, all these facts will have a common shape or pattern; but this is not a separable entity that 'subsists', for a function is precisely *not* separable from its arguments and values. Even if we acknowledge the numbers mentioned in '120 is the factorial of 6' as identifiable entities, we shall not need to recognize the Factorial as a further entity, and may well not feel any temptation to do so.

Numbers, however, form a much more important *prima facie* exception to McTaggart's thesis that whatever is, is actual. In surface grammar, predications about numbers and predications (say) about people are very similar: compare, '2 is even, prime, and greater than 1' with, 'John is bald, fat, and younger than Tom'. A follower of Frege might say that if '1' and '2' behave in every way as though they were proper names, then they are proper names. We can identify individual numbers and count kinds of numbers just as we can identify individual men and count kinds of men. We can indeed speak of pictures of numbers: the number 3 is more readily identifiable from the picture ❘ * * * ❘ than a criminal is from a police photograph, and both sorts of picture depend for their use on our learning a convention. Nor does the criterion of identity for a number generate more philosophical puzzles than that of a person. So a strong case may be made out for regarding numbers as individual objects. If so, we must regard them as non-actual objects, not as existent objects or substances; for unless we go in for the gross superstitions about lucky and unlucky numbers, numbers are causally inefficacious; they cannot initiate change nor can they undergo change; they have no share in the activity of the world. How McTaggart would have replied to a Fregean defence of the thesis that numbers are non-actual individuals, must remain a matter of mere conjecture.

Appeal to facts enabled McTaggart, he thought, to dispense not only with *universalia ante res*, but also with Propositions. We need not characterize two beliefs 'in the same thing' by their having the same Proposition as their object, for we could just as easily say that if true they both agree with, and if false they

both *disagree* with, the same fact. So Propositions appear superfluous for explaining truth and falsehood of beliefs, and beliefs'
being 'in the same thing'; and false Propositions appear specially
objectionable; they are one form of philosophical monsters that
McTaggart was eager to slay – objectified falsehoods or errors
or fictions detached from an erring or feigning subject.

There is moreover another thing wrong with the notion, in its
modern guise and equally in the old guise of the Stoic *lekton* or
the medieval *enuntiabile*: there is a confusion between a unitary
bit of *information* and a unit of *meaning*. This comes out in the
sort of explanation we often find in those elementary logic books
which use the notion of Propositions. On the one hand, it is
Propositions that are supposed to be true or false in the primary
sense: beliefs, sentences, etc. would be true or false according to
the truth or falsehood of some corresponding Proposition. But
on the other hand we are likely to be told some such thing as
that the sentences, 'It is raining', '*Il pleut*', and, '*Es regnet*' all
express the same Proposition: they are indeed intertranslatable,
but a moment's thought shows that to this common *meaning*
there does not attach any fixed assignment of truth or falsehood.
The sentences, 'A bomb exploded in London today', said on
Monday, and, 'A bomb exploded in London yesterday', said on
Tuesday, *will* have the same truth-value, and may well be said
to give the same *information*; Frege would say they both express
the same thought (*Gedanke*), the difference in the words used
compensating for the difference in time of utterance. But then
this piece of information cannot be identified with the Proposition as object of belief or thought; for if a man is somehow
muddled about the passage of time he may easily react to one
sentence with belief and to the other with incredulity. I conclude
that the idea of Propositions as a class of non-actual entities is
thoroughly confused.

McTaggart's rejection of possibilities as entities distinct from
the actual world will be clearly understandable only when we
come on to his account of determination in Chapter 4. As we
shall see, he there takes a very restrictive view even of the possibilities inherent in things that do actually exist. But the aspects
of his thought already presented in this chapter should make

readers accurately anticipate what he thinks about possibilities supposedly independent of actuality and anterior to it. He rejects out of hand the idea of such possibilities. That e.g. a red triangle is possible would be a matter of triangular shape's *not* implying the absence of redness; and such facts about which characteristics are or are not implied by others, like the characteristics involved in the facts, are rooted only in actuality. The extravagances of recent possible-worlds theorizing would have been castigated by McTaggart, just as he castigated those who spoke of reality in the world of some novel.

3 Individuals and characteristics

McTaggart has thus set the stage for us; we have a world of actuality standing there by itself, not surrounded by any un-realities like *possibilia* or fictitious beings, and not dependent either on any non-actual Platonic world of numbers or universals. Characteristics are real only by being actual, only by being in-volved in actual facts; and they are thus involved even in facts of their own non-instantiation. To borrow a neat way of put-ting the matter from Wittgenstein: even if a thing, *B* say, is not red, *red* is in that case what *B* isn't. We have not done with possibilities; we shall return to them in the chapter on determin-acy and determination (Chapter 4), to see how McTaggart fits in some of our talk about possibilities into his system and would have us reject other parts of it as simply a kind of nonsense we are inclined to talk.

Within this world we have to recognize what McTaggart calls substances. His use of the term 'substance' may well appear odd; his own reply to such a comment would be that he gives the term a traditional sense, and differs from other philosophers in its application only because of their inconsistency. Certainly his use has long historical roots, via medieval philosophy, in Aristotle's conception of *prōtē ousia*; like Aristotle, he is concerned with that which is primarily actual, that from which all other actuality derives. McTaggart's substances, characteristics, and facts have a non-trivial correspondence respectively with *prōtai ousiai*, forms, and individual accidents in Aristotle.

The definition of substance given in 67 is corrected by a MS note in McTaggart's own copy of the work, so that his final definition of substance amounts to this: A substance is some-thing that has characteristics but is itself neither a characteristic nor a fact. Since substances have characteristics, there will be facts about any substance – the facts that it has this, that, and the other characteristic; but a substance is not itself a fact. For anything to be actual, there must be fixed starting-points of actuality; there cannot be characteristics of characteristics of characteristics . . . , or facts about facts about facts . . . , or facts about characteristics of facts about characteristics . . . , or anything of the sort, that would give us an unattached chain of dependence running on to infinity. Finally, we *must* come to that which is primarily actual, that which has characteristics and has facts holding about it but is not a characteristic or a fact. This is the way McTaggart argues for the necessity that there be substances; it is closely allied to the way Wittgenstein argues in the *Tractatus* that there must be *objects* that are the *substance* of the world (2.0201–0202; 4.2211).

The big difference between McTaggart's substances and Wittgenstein's objects is that the latter are supposed to be simple, incomposite, whereas the former need not be. (In fact, we shall see that for McTaggart *no* substance is simple.) Wittgenstein held that what is complex is always a fact: the existence of the complex is to be identified with the holding of some constitutive structural relation between individuals. If we are not to have facts about facts about facts . . . *ad infinitum*, the individuals about which facts hold must not themselves always be complexes, which are facts; in the end we must come to individual entities which are not facts and which are simple, devoid of internal structure; the way certain simple objects stand to one another is what constitutes any complex object of ordinary experience.

Wittgenstein's view is certainly in part attributable to a confusion between two senses of a phrase like '*A* above *B*': it may signify the fact that *A* is above *B*, or signify a whole made up of *A* and *B*, in which, as it happens, *A* is above *B*. When Russell used such a phrase he would use hyphens, '*A*-above-*B*', with the effect of muddling himself about this distinction. Is 'Alexander-on-Bucephalus' to be read as standing for a physical whole – Bucephalus, Alexander up – such as a sculptor might represent by carving one block of marble? Or is it to mean the fact that Alexander is on Bucephalus? McTaggart was wholly free from this confusion that Wittgenstein shared with Russell: so he was not impelled to say that the substances that have facts about them, but are not themselves facts, must be simple. Indeed, as we shall see, he believed he could discern *a priori* that *every* substance has an internal structure, and has parts that are likewise substances.

McTaggart holds by a conception of substance that has often been assailed in the history of philosophy. Opponents of the conception will say, 'Granting for the sake of argument that the substance *A* has such-and-such characteristics and is not a characteristic, what then *is* the substance *A*?' They have of course rigged the question-and-answer game so that no answer given by the friend of substance will be acceptable; the question is an invitation to predicate something of *A*, and yet any actual predication concerning *A* will be met with: 'That only gives us a quality or relation of *A*; what we wanted to know is what *A* as a substance *is*.' On these terms the defender of substance can of course not say anything; and this reduction to silence is treated as a triumphant *reductio ad absurdum* of the conception of substance.

One way out that people attempt is to identify a substance with a bundle of characteristics; another way is to say that underlying the qualities and relations of any substance *A* there is a 'bare particular' *A'*, which, just because it is to play this role of underlying and supporting the qualities and relations of *A*, itself has no qualities and stands in no relations. Both these attempted answers rest upon thinking of a substance and its characteristics by comparison to a very gross picture: a much bedizened lady and her clothes. One party is saying, as the little girl is alleged to have hinted to her mother, that the lady is 'clothes all the way through', without any flesh that you come to in the end: the other party is saying (and indeed this very expression is to be found in philosophical writing on the subject) that if we 'mentally strip off' the characteristics of *A* we come to the 'bare particular' *A'*. They have in mind what would happen if we literally stripped clothes off a lady.

Both ways of thinking are really absurd, indeed are not ways of thinking at all but a mere play of words set off by an irrelevant image. Since we never meet with ladies who are clothes all the way through, but on the contrary know that if you actually did strip off all the clothes you'd get a naked lady, the theory of bare particulars has an appeal that the theory of characteristics tied together with one another has never had (in spite of Bertrand Russell's attempt to make something of it). There are a number of pseudo-concepts introduced at different critical points in philosophy, to solve different problems or apparent problems, all having a strong family resemblance:

In the make-up of each individual thing there must be a bare particular, which has no qualities or relations precisely because it is the subject of inherence for these characteristics.

In any process of change there must be some changeless element, to act as a substratum of the process of change.

What I really mean by 'I' is something simple, with no mental states in its make-up like my empirical self: it is my *pure ego*, which stands to my mental states in the peculiar relation of ownership.

And finally the Scholastic theory of *materia prima*:

If the same stuff in a bottle is now wine, now vinegar, this is because there is prime matter underlying now the form of wine, now the form of vinegar; this prime matter does not *have* the form of wine or vinegar, rather it is all the time devoid of any form.

As regards this theory the picture of the bedizened lady comes quickly to the surface of the mind, as in Butler's description of his antihero's philosophical ability in *Hudibras*:

He had first matter seen undressed,
Taken her naked all alone
Before one rag of form was on.

I count it as a great good fortune that a reading of McTaggart when I was a teenager inoculated me for life against these various mutations of a metaphysical virus. In every case we have a conjoint assertion and denial, the negative member of which uses some piece of jargon; and either the jargon is meaningless, or the two conjuncts are flatly contradictory. I have mental states: my *pure ego* does not have them but *owns* them. A thing

B changes, or undergoes change: but there must be in *B* something that does not change but is a *substratum presupposed* to the change. And so on. People will even say, with the air of making things clear, that it is *just because* the substratum is *presupposed* to change that it undergoes no change, *just because* the bare particular is the *subject* or *bearer* of characteristics that it has no characteristics, etc., etc.! But either 'being a subject or bearer of characteristics' and 'being a substratum presupposed to change' are blown-up technical variants for 'having characteristics' and 'undergoing change', or they are mere nonsense; and if we drop the jargon, then as I said we have flat self-contradiction, e.g. that a thing undergoes no change precisely because it does undergo change. To be sure, some people are so hypnotized by mere words that even without jargon they will think to avoid contradiction by change of the stress: 'A substance can have no *qualities* because *it* is *what has* the qualities'!

It will help us to get into the healthy frame of mind that eschews all this nonsense if we shift to a better picture than that of the bedizened lady. We do much better to compare a substance and its characteristics to a triangle (I mean a triangular area) and its sides. A triangle is delimited by its periphery, and apart from that would be nothing at all; but it cannot be identified with its sides, either severally or jointly.

Clearly there could not be two triangles with the same three sides. Analogously, there could not be two substances with just the same set of characteristics; the characteristics of a substance determine which substance it is. This leads us to the principle McTaggart calls the Dissimilarity of the Diverse; denial of this appears to proceed from some hankering after the bedizened lady – the body under the clothes could be exchanged for another even if the change did not show in any way. Without such nonsense at the back of our minds, there is no reason why we should not accept the principle. It is best known in philosophy by Leibniz's name, the Identity of Indiscernibles; this, as McTaggart remarks, misleadingly suggests that there are indiscernibles, in the plural, but these stand in an identity-relation! McTaggart's name is much better. The principle itself was clearly formulated by Aquinas: that whatever things differ, differ *secundum aliquam affirmationem et negationem*, differ because something is truly predicable of one and not of the other. Predication itself is not paradoxical, nor can we escape from it; to try to think without predicating is like trying to wash without wetting your skin. I think McTaggart was completely right in rejecting any mystery-mongering about this. We say what a substance is, we show which substance we are talking about, by characterizing the substance; but although substances are thus identified *by* their characteristics, they are not to be identified *with* their characteristics, even taken all together for each substance.

A characteristic is most clearly located in McTaggart's system if we borrow on his behalf the notion of a function as Frege and Wittgenstein conceived it. A fact about an individual's being characterized in such-and-such a way will then be the value, for some individual substance as argument, of a definite function, and we may identify the characteristic with this function. Redness, say, will be a function whose values, for red objects A, B, C as arguments, are the redness of A, the redness of B, the redness of C; and these last, for McTaggart, will be facts.

McTaggart accepted from the contemporary Cambridge jargon a simple dichotomy of characteristics into qualities and relations: any characteristic expressed by a one-place predicate is a quality. This is a drastic simplification of the Aristotelian categories, cutting the list down by omission of several members; it is odd even in modern ears, because traces of the Aristotelian tradition still persist, to call being a man, or being fourteen stone in weight, or standing, or singing, a *quality* of a man. I am here merely recording McTaggart's usage.

Relations were traditionally spoken of as relations *of* something *to* something; they had a subject of inherence *whose* relations they were, and termini *to which* they related the subject. In McTaggart's Cambridge the shibboleth of orthodoxy was, not to say this, but to speak of relations' being *between* things; but McTaggart, like the men of Ephraim, could not quite manage to pronounce the shibboleth right.[1] This is entirely to his credit. For replacing the old jargon with the new 'between' jargon does

[1] See *Judges* 12:6.

not make the distinctive trait of relations clear, but quite the reverse. If A is spatially between B and C, A is between C and B; so use of the 'between' jargon blurs one of the most important traits of relations, lack of symmetry. If C is R to B, B need not be R to C; this is not clarified but obscured by saying, 'R may hold between C and B but not between B and C.'

Nor is this idea of relations' not inhering in substances needed for a workable logic of relations. On the contrary, the standard predicate calculus presupposes that all the instances of 'Qag', 'a is Q to g', are also instances of 'Fa'; if we were not allowed to pass from a valid schema in which '$F*$' occurred (I use an asterisk here as a place-holder for a name or name-variable) to one in which '$Q*g$' was uniformly substituted, standard predicate logic would collapse. The view that relational propositions *cannot* be treated as predications concerning the related things whose names there occur is so far from being presupposed in modern predicate logic, that its contrary is presupposed, namely that any such proposition *can* thus be formally treated as predicative. The point needs some emphasis because the wrong theory has often been stated in a degenerate logical tradition stemming from Russell, in which writers mistakenly thought that they understood *Principia Mathematica*, and is even perhaps to be found in the philosophical journalism of Russell himself.

If we turn from formal logic to ontology, we can see that there too there is absolutely no need for the idea of relations 'between' things rather than inherent in things. Here once more an idea inspired by Frege and by Wittgenstein's *Tractatus*, that we should identify a universal with a function, helps us to spell the matter out very plainly. We have seen that what McTaggart calls qualities will be one-argument functions whose arguments are individual substances $A, B, C, \ldots$ and whose values are (say) A's whiteness, B's whiteness, C's whiteness . . . , all of these being facts. But now we can say that a relational characteristic, say *being son of*, is a function whose values for arguments $A, B, C, \ldots$ are not facts but (in the sense just explained) qualities: being son of A, being son of B, being son of C. . . . Each of these qualities is again a function, whose values for individual substances as arguments are facts: thus, the function or quality

(McTaggart calls it a relational quality) *being son of David* will have as its values for Absalom, Amnon, Nathan, and Solomon as arguments the facts concerning each of these that he is a son of David. That Solomon, say, is son of David is one of these four facts; it is the value for the argument Solomon of the function *being son of David*; and this relational quality, itself a function, is at the same time the value of the function *being son of* for David as argument. We have no need to bring in obscure jargon about the relation *being son of* as being 'between' Solomon and David, nor need we wonder why then it is not 'between' David and Solomon. And we see exactly how relations, relational qualities, and facts ought to be taken as standing to each other. McTaggart, trying with imperfect success to talk the 'between' language, recognized as distinct facts the fact that Solomon has the relational quality *being son of David*, and the fact that the sonship relation holds between Solomon and David; but there was no need for him to do so.

The degenerate tradition to which I have referred sometimes taught that the sentence 'Solomon is son of David' admits of logical dissection *only* into the two proper names and the relative term 'is son of', and that accordingly there is no logically viable cutting 'is son of David' to which would correspond a relational property *being son of David*. (For one presentation of this, notably vigorous in style, see Frank Ramsey's essay on 'Universals'.) But the premise of the argument is false: it is false that in logic '* is son of David' does not show a way of forming sentences out of names. The metaphysical objection: 'How *can* an individual like David be part of a universal *being son of David*?' fares no better than the logical one. The name 'David' is part of the string of words 'is son of David', but it is mere confusion to suppose that a similar relation must relate what is signified by these expressions.

As I said, McTaggart's principle of the Dissimilarity of the Diverse appears to me a necessary part of his doctrine of substance. A substance in abstraction from its characteristics is as much of an absurdity as a triangle in abstraction from its sides; and just as there cannot be two triangular areas, on a plane or spherical surface, with the same periphery, so there cannot be two substances with the same set of characteristics. From this principle McTaggart thinks he can infer what on the face of it is a much stronger principle: the principle of Sufficient Description. Not only must every pair of substances differ in at least one attribute: every substance must have a characteristic belonging to it and it alone that could be expressed in purely general terms, without using the proper name of any substance. 'Father of Julius Caesar' is an *exclusive* description, which can belong to only one substance, but the use of the name 'Julius Caesar' means that this is not a *sufficient* description.

It is not very difficult to imagine systems of description by which e.g. each human being would have a sufficient description. It is supposed that any two men have distinct fingerprints: a system of description that allowed all fingerprints to be uniquely identified would afford a sufficient description of each human being. Again, suppose that all human beings are descendants of Adam and Eve. Adam and Eve would then have the sufficient descriptions 'the first man' and 'the first woman'; Cain would have the sufficient description 'the first son of the first man and the first woman'; and given a genealogical tree of the human race such sufficient descriptions could be constructed for each of us. Of course the descriptions would soon become too long and complex for a human mind to take in; but since McTaggart's thesis is not epistemological this is irrelevant. He is maintaining that there must *be* sufficient descriptions for individuals to *be* distinct, not that we must grasp the descriptions in order to distinguish things.

Let us now consider McTaggart's argument for the principle. It goes like this. Take first any individual substance A. A, by the Dissimilarity of the Diverse, must have an exclusive description; if this description is purely in terms of non-relational properties, or if it is in terms of relational properties specified by means of sufficient descriptions instead of names (e.g. 'first son of the first man and the first woman'), then we are home already with a sufficient description of A. But suppose the exclusive description of A is 'being R to B'. The relational characteristic of being R to B can itself be distinct from the characteristics of being R to F, being R to G, etc. only if the individuation of B is secured;

and by the Dissimilarity of the Diverse B too will need an exclusive description. The argument then repeats as regards B: if B has a sufficient description, so does A – the description 'being R to something that is XYZ', if 'XYZ' represents a sufficient description of A; if on the contrary B's exclusive description comes from B's being in the relation S to C, the characteristic of being S to C will be a definite characteristic only if C's being an identifiable individual is presupposed. So now we consider the exclusive description of C. . . . This series can come to an end with a 'House that Jack Built' definite description if one of the substances A, B, C, . . . has a sufficient description 'XYZ', which gives us 'being R to something that is S to . . . to something that is XYZ' as what we need to turn A's exclusive description into a sufficient one; or alternatively the complex relation expressed by 'being R to something that is S to something that is T to . . .' might itself become so rare that only A bore it to anything at all, and then again we have a sufficient description (104).

Thus far McTaggart has only shown ways in which a substance *could* have a sufficient description. The crucial step in his argument is the attempt to show that we cannot here have an infinite series A, B, C, . . . , of individuals with exclusive but not sufficient descriptions. To repeat: the supposed relation between consecutive terms in the series, say A and B, is that A is individuated by some relation to B, and this individuating characteristic will itself be a definite characteristic only if the individuation of B is already given. If this relation is supposed to generate an infinite series, A's individuating characteristics depend for their identity on the individuation of B, and B's individuating characteristics on the individuation of C, and so on without end: the individuating characteristics for any term in the series thus have a fixed identity only if the series has an end, but *ex hypothesi* it has none. So McTaggart concludes that the series cannot be endless; but if it comes to an end, then as we saw, each term in the series has a sufficient description (105).

Broad has pointed out one oversight in this proof: McTaggart tacitly assumes that the list 'A, B, C, . . .' is non-repetitive, whereas there is nothing in the logic of the argument to exclude our coming back to another name of a substance already listed. But the gap is easily filled up: repetition in the list would merely give us a vicious circle instead of a vicious infinite regress, if we supposed that a substance can have an exclusive but no sufficient description. Let us take the simplest case: suppose that 'admirer of *A*' or 'pitier of *A*' is an exclusive description of *A*. Broad is of course right in saying that this could be so even though 'admirer of himself' or 'pitier of himself' were not an exclusive description of *A*: for although '*A* admires *A*' is logically equivalent to '*A* admires himself', '*A* is the only admirer of *A*' and '*A* is the only self-admirer' are not equivalent. But could it be true that the *only* feature to individuate *A* was: being an admirer of *A*, or: being a pitier of *A*? Surely not; the identity of such relational characteristics depends on the individuation of *A*, and they therefore cannot serve to individuate *A*. If *A*'s individuation depended on the characteristic *pitier of A*, but the identity of this characteristic depended on the individuation of *A*, we should run in a vicious circle. Similarly for more complicated cases; e.g. if *A* had the exclusive description 'being *R* to *B*' and *B* had the exclusive description 'being *S* to *A*', we should run in a vicious circle if we supposed these descriptions to give the *only* ways of individuating *A* and *B*.

We may see clearly the absurdity of Broad's position if we consider another imaginary case he constructs to show the possibility of exclusive descriptions without any sufficient descriptions. Broad imagines a set-up in which nothing exists but what we may call an unholy trinity: there are three persons *A*, *B*, and *C* between whom the only difference is that *A* is jealous of *B* on account of *C*, *B* is jealous of *C* on account of *A*, and *C* is jealous of *A* on account of *B*. Otherwise *A*, *B*, and *C* are entirely alike: as theologians say of the Blessed Trinity, so also in Broad's unblessed trinity, everything is the same for all the persons except for the opposition of relations. The relation of jealousy involves three distinct persons; and it is clear that e.g. 'being jealous of *B* on account of *C*' will in the case supposed be an exclusive description of *A*, not shared by *B* and *C*. *B* and *C* will each have a similar exclusive description, not shared by the other two persons. And Broad supposes that these exclusive descriptions could be enough to differentiate the three persons, even though none of them had any sufficient description.

It is worth remarking that this trinity of persons distinguished by relations alone is even more incomprehensible than the Blessed Trinity. For though e.g. the Father and the Son are distinguished just by their mutual relations, Christians do not say that as the Father is father of the Son, so the Son is father of the Father; as the Athanasian symbol says, there is only one Father, not three fathers; 'being a father' would be an exclusive description of one Divine Person, and indeed a *sufficient* description, if nothing else existed besides the Trinity. But in Broad's trinity the persons cannot be thus differentiated: each is both subject, object, and occasion of their internecine jealousy, reminiscent of Lytton Strachey's Bloomsbury.

Once again, it appears that the supposedly distinguishing characteristics, e.g. *being jealous of A on account of B* and *being jealous of B on account of C*, can themselves be definite characteristics only if the individuation of *A*, *B*, and *C* is supposed already given: these characteristics cannot serve to individuate *A*, *B*, and *C*. Broad thinks that he can (as Descartes would say) see very clearly and distinctly that his unblessed trinity could be all that exists. I can only reply that I see very clearly and distinctly that Broad is talking through his hat; and there I leave it.

I conclude that we ought to accept McTaggart's principle of Sufficient Description as a correct inference from the Dissimilarity of the Diverse, and therefore as necessarily true. McTaggart, like Wittgenstein in the *Tractatus*, is committed to the view that the Universe could be *completely* described in completely general terms, with no irreducible use of a 'non-connotative' proper name; and I think this view ought to be accepted.

4 Determinacy and determination

The topics of this chapter both relate to the characteristics of substances. It is a fault in McTaggart's presentation that the topic of determinacy comes much later in the book than it should: instead of coming in the early discussions about substances and characteristics, it is suddenly introduced in the course of discussing intricate difficulties about parts within parts to infinity (Chapter XXIII, 'The Contradiction of Infinite Divisibility'). That is not the only fault of presentation. Quite ill-advisedly, McTaggart stated his principle by using the word 'presupposition' in a new technical sense; this terminology only obscures the principle; and in view of the huge amount that has been written by philosophers and linguists about 'presuppositions' in a wholly different sense (as when one says that the question 'Has Jim been happier since his wife died?' has a presupposition that Jim was married) I think I could not keep to McTaggart's way of speaking without grave risk of confusion. I shall instead speak of the principle of Ontological Determinacy: the adjective is meant to distinguish, but bring together, this principle and another principle we shall come to later, the principle of Perceptual Determinacy. The principle is: Nothing can have a determinable characteristic without having it in a perfectly determinate form. For example, nothing can have shape without having a perfectly determinate shape, or size without having a perfectly determinate size, or colour without having a perfectly determinate colour. Vagueness and fuzziness can infect only our descriptions, not the actual things we describe.

Whereas under McTaggart's eccentric label ('Total Ultimate Presupposition'!) this principle may look peculiar to him, it is in fact one shared by him with very many philosophers and has played an enormous role in the history of philosophy. I believe, though this raises tricky questions of interpretation, that this principle underlies Aristotle's difficult discussion of the law of non-contradiction as an ontological principle. Certainly the principle is to be found in Berkeley, and even more explicitly in Hume; it is frequently appealed to in the writings of Bertrand Russell. It played a particularly important part in Wittgenstein's thinking: for the young Wittgenstein, in the *Notebooks* and the *Tractatus*, it was a guideline; for the older Wittgenstein it was a dangerous snare against which people engaged in philosophy must be explicitly warned. He once gave this example: A prisoner in a dungeon must have a quite definite bit of space assigned to him; no doubt the walls that enclose him will be somewhat elastic, not perfectly rigid, but then they must have a perfectly definite degree of elasticity! Comical as this sounds, we must realize that it is no parody of the principle, but a spelling out of its concrete consequences.

It is easy to think of a determinable predicate like '(chromatically) coloured' as short for a disjunction of more determinate predicates, 'red or orange or yellow . . .'. Obviously if we have a disjunction, even though some of its disjuncts may themselves be disjunctions, we must come in the end to simple disjuncts that are not disjunctions. So if 'coloured' is spelled out as 'either red or orange or . . .', and 'red' in turn is spelled out as 'either crimson or vermilion or magenta or . . .', and so on, must we not come in the end to some colour-predicate that cannot be further expanded into a disjunction? So must not the series of characteristics: chromatically coloured, red, magenta, . . . terminate in some completely determinate colour, even if we have no word for this; and will not this hold even if the number of fully determinate colours is infinite?

It is this last consideration that ought to give us pause. It is not obvious that the difference between a finite and listable set of alternatives, and a case where indefinitely fine discriminations are possible, *is* logically trivial: that we can dismiss it as a matter of the logically irrelevant 'medical impossibility' (to borrow a term from Russell) of a human being's getting through an infinite list in a finite time. Nor upon consideration does it seem to me obvious that such a series of characteristics as: chromatically coloured, red, magenta, . . . must always terminate in a last term or limit that admits of no finer discriminations. In Mc-Taggart's Cambridge there prevailed the opinion that any such doubts about the transition from finite to infinite cases were the vulgar errors of those who had not learned Cantor's theory of transfinite cardinal numbers; and he was in this matter a man of his time and place. But when we see the devastating consequences that McTaggart inferred from the principle of Ontological Determinacy, our doubts may be reinforced.

McTaggart's ideas of extrinsic and intrinsic determination are perhaps most easily understood in relation to causality. Many philosophers allow that for causality more is needed than a mere true generalization: e.g. it seems that for it to be true that beheading a man causes his death it must be true not only that any man who is beheaded forthwith dies, but also that any men who *were* beheaded *would* forthwith die. But these subjunctive conditionals are no less problematic than causality itself.

How superficial philosophical thought about causality often is in our day comes out in the way that philosophers think of a causal law as saying that an event of type X is regularly followed by an event of type Y. In any causal law that we need take seriously, something more than mere temporal succession will be specified as relating cause and effect: e.g. that the beheading of a human body is followed by the almost immediate death *of the same body*, or that lightning is followed by thunder *at an interval in proportion to the distance of the lightning*. This point was made by McTaggart in his treatment of causal laws, but is generally neglected in contemporary treatments, even when they make a show of precision. Donald Davidson, for example, introduces no special relation (such as the ones indicated above by the words in italics) apart from temporal succession, but tries to make this precise by specifying *what time-interval* there must be between cause and effect; this specification is not only insufficient, it may well be positively wrong; as in the example of lightning and thunder, where the interval is variable.

McTaggart held that one characteristic non-logically implies another, and called this non-logical implication 'intrinsic determination'; and he held that it is quite irrational to believe in any causal generalization unless we also believe that an intrinsic determination is involved. I shall discuss these two theses in order.

The thesis that there are intrinsic determinations of characteristics is the same as the thesis that there are non-logical or synthetic incompatibilities of characteristics: for X's intrinsically determining Y is the same as X's being incompatible with the absence of Y, and X's being incompatible with Z is the same as X's intrinsically determining the absence of Z. Now how should we regard, e.g., the incompatibility between red and green? Strawson has argued that this sort of incompatibility is verbal and man-made: *men* decide on a practice never to *call* the same thing 'red' and 'green'. We should not be readily persuaded that this view is correct. For men's ability to adopt such a practice depends upon the fact that no phoneme-sequence that is an instance of the word 'red' is also an instance of the word 'green', that instances of these two words always sound quite differently. But why should we be confident of that? That no human utterance is an instance both of the word 'red' and of the word 'green' depends on the very same sort of contrast and incompatibility between sensible characteristics that we were trying to explain away in the instance, 'Nothing can be red and green all over'; our decision never to use the two words for the same coloured patch depends upon an incompatibility not itself created by convention. If two words have nearly the same sound, a decision never to apply them to the same thing is going to be futile; our Anglo-Saxon ancestors were surely in bad trouble through having two words sounding nearly the same, one meaning 'black' and one meaning 'white' (cf. the *Oxford English Dictionary* s.v. 'black' and 'blake'), and naturally one of the two words (the word for 'white') went out of use. So the idea that there are synthetic incompatibilities of qualities, and by the same token intrinsic determinations, is not so easily dismissed as some people suppose.

McTaggart argues that only in terms of intrinsic determinations can we make sense of what *would* have happened in some non-actual set-up. If the characteristic of being a human body that has just been beheaded intrinsically determines the characteristic of being a moribund human body, then we can make sense of the statement, 'If Charles II had been beheaded, Charles II would forthwith have died.' But can we make sense otherwise of the question what characteristics a substance, say Charles II, *would* have had on a certain hypothesis? McTaggart thinks not: unless there is something *following by necessity* from the characteristics ascribed to Charles II on the false hypothesis, there is simply no saying what he *would* have been like on that hypothesis. So if we make it part of the import of a causal law that there should be subjunctive conditionals following from it, we must take the law to state an intrinsic determination: for example, if we take the causal law that connects beheading and death to imply the subjunctive conditional just stated about Charles II, then we must believe that beheading intrinsically determines death.

A little reflection may shake any confidence about understanding subjunctive conditionals in any other way. How can we ask what would *in fact* have happened in a case where *ex hypothesi* there are no actual facts? What would actually have happened if Napoleon had won at Waterloo? All sorts of things *might* have happened, surely; he might have been shot after the victory by a Prussian soldier, or he might have died of cancer in his fifties, or. . . . With regard to the real world, we can ask what definitely did happen after Napoleon lost; but except in so far as we have intrinsic determinations by which to derive consequences from the false supposition that Napoleon won, there is simply no way of picking out of these various possibilities the one giving us 'what *actually would* have happened to Napoleon'.

In late Scholasticism there was much discussion about how men *would* have acted by free choice in circumstances that never arose; such *futuribilia*, depending as they did on free choice, would not be mappable by any causal laws applied to antecedent events. God however was supposed to know these *futuribilia*; and some men even supposed they know enough about Divine Providence to know that God's ordering of the world, in particular his dispensation of grace, depended on his knowledge of what men would have freely done in circumstances that God knew would never arise. We may smile at the vanity of such

speculations, or deplore their profaneness; but modern speculations about possible worlds are really no better.

McTaggart argues for an even tougher doctrine on the basis
of his view of substance and characteristics. Let us revert to the
useful simile of the triangle and its sides, to which I resorted in
discussing the Dissimilarity of the Diverse. A substance is determined by its characteristics in much the way that a triangle is by
its periphery. Now, 'There could be two triangles with the same
periphery' and 'There could have been this very triangle with a
different periphery, with sides of different lengths and propor-
tions' strike one as similarly and equally absurd. And so does
McTaggart regard as similarly and equally absurd these two
propositions: 'There could be two substances with the very same
set of characteristics' and 'There could be this very substance
with a different set of characteristics.' A substance, in McTaggart's view, unites its characteristics like the awkward sort of
key-ring from which you cannot remove one key without getting
them all off. You have no right to say 'I am only assuming the
absence of one piddling little characteristic; I can surely assume
that any others will remain, unless its absence carries their
absence with it by intrinsic determination.' Not at all, McTaggart
would reply: in removing the most insignificant characteristic
by a counterfactual supposition, you remove the substance that
is the bond of unity of the characteristics, and instead of what
would then remain you have only the boundless combinations of
characteristics compatible with logical and causal laws. An
enormous variety of descriptions *might* have been instantiated;
from among these you have no right to pick one description as
giving what definitely *would* have existed on your contrafactual
supposition. 'To ask what would happen, or what would remain
in the universe, if I had sneezed yesterday once less than I did
sneeze, is as hopeless and unprofitable as it would be to ask
what would happen, or what would remain in the universe, if
twice three were seven, or if things which are equal to the same
thing were not equal to one another' (139).

McTaggart thus holds that the possession of any characteristic
by a given substance A is indissolubly linked to the possession
of any other: even if some other substance B is X without being

Y, that does not license us to say *A* could have been *X* without being *Y*. This linkage between all the facts about a given substance McTaggart calls Extrinsic Determination. Extrinsic determination relates all individual facts about substances in the Universe; to people who do not like the idea of a 'block' Universe, McTaggart replies that that is just too bad: this is the way the Universe is and cannot but be (143).

5 Parts and wholes

McTaggart was one of the least linguistic of philosophers: he adverts to the use of words very little. I am far from thinking that what has been called 'the linguistic turn' is always good for the solution of philosophical problems: all too often, the problem supposedly dissolved by an appeal to language replicates itself on the level of language – not surprisingly, because language is part of the world, not something contrasting with the world. For example, we cannot dismiss the problem of universals by saying it is an illusion due to our applying one *word* to many things; for the relation between *the* word 'sheep' (as we say) and its many utterances is another case of that relation between the Sheep and the many sheep which we were trying to avoid discussing. Again, as we saw, the problem of synthetic incompatibilities cannot be disposed of by the linguistic turn: the same problem arises about incompatible sound-qualities in our utterances. So upon the whole I think McTaggart's not going in for language about language did him little harm.

However, in the present chapter I think something of a linguistic turn is needed. McTaggart fell into error through neglect of the actual functioning of language in this region of discourse. The notions with which we are here concerned are very deep rooted in human language (specially English idioms are not important); and I think Russell was right in his *Principles of Mathematics* in urging that close attention to language, e.g. to our use of plurals and lists, has much to teach us in logic and philosophy. In that work he tried to practise what he preached; but in later work on set theory he lost this clue and regarded such investigations with manifest contempt. How careless in thought he then became can be exemplified from the introduction to *Principia Mathematica*, where he tells us that the sentences

'A whale is big' and, 'One is a number' look alike (sc. grammatically) but are logically different; but the two would after all be treated quite differently even in high-school grammar, let alone in scientific linguistics. Like Wittgenstein, I find the *aporiai* of the *Principles* much more instructive than the solutions that the later work purports to give. And it is to the earlier work that we need to turn for a good understanding of what McTaggart says about groups and wholes.

To begin with groups: McTaggart uses the term 'group' in very much the same way as Russell uses the term 'collection' or 'class as many': namely, for what is supposed to correspond *in rebus* to a list of proper names; the items of the list will name individual substances that are members of the group (120).

To answer the question what does thus correspond *in rebus* to a list, we need first to consider the logical syntax of lists. A list is understandable only in the context of a sentence; an examining board's list may perhaps not supply such a context explicitly, but may be taken as implying such a context as, 'The following candidates passed such-and-such an examination: . . . .' Further, the context of a list will be one in which there can occur without disturbance of syntax (*salva congruitate* as medieval logicians say) either one name or several names: in a bad year the examiners might have only one successful candidate to list.

Let us consider the example, 'Only———— had a chance to steal the ruby.' We may fill the blank with a single name, 'Bill', or with a list of names joined by 'and' or 'or': 'Only Bill or Tom . . .', 'Only Bill and Tom . . .'. And we *can* use the sentences with lists in them so that the choice of 'and' or 'or' does not make any odds; not as regards the truth-conditions, that is. 'Only Bill or Tom . . .' might suggest that if Bill had a chance Tom didn't, and, 'Only Bill and Tom . . .' might on the contrary suggest that they had a chance to do the job together: but these are only suggestions, and here as elsewhere it is a big mistake to read into the truth-conditions of a sentence something that the sentence suggests, or that would normally be true when a man made a serious assertoric use of the sentence to tell the truth. I leave aside for the moment the reading of 'Only Bill and Tom . . .' to mean that nobody had a chance to steal the ruby except Bill and

Tom *as a team*; I shall return to such collective predications shortly. At any rate there is *a* reading of the sentence with 'and', and *a* reading of the sentence with 'or', that give the two sentences exactly the same truth-condition: 'and' and 'or' are then logically mere interjections, all that matters logically being the list of names joined by these particles (and the order of the list is again logically indifferent).

Such a list has on the face of it the role of a logical subject. Misled by the way predications can be made with a list as subject, McTaggart inferred that to a list there corresponds *in rebus* something that has characteristics and about which there are facts, but which is neither a characteristic nor a fact: a substance, and in particular a 'group'. Russell was a little more cautious: he introduced the general term 'collection' for what corresponds *in rebus* to a list, but with the explicit warning that *a* collection is not something single: a collection for him is *things*, not *a* thing. But both Russell and McTaggart regarded groups or collections as bearers of characteristics, of numerical characteristics in particular: *A*, *B*, and *C*, let us say, *are three* (122).

On this matter I think they both made a fundamental mistake, repeatedly attacked by Frege. Frege is surely right in saying that an assignment of number (*Zahlangabe*) attaches not to some plurality of named objects, but to a *kind* of things: in his jargon, to a *Begriff*. In controversy with Husserl, Frege mentioned an example that has not ceased to be topical: he posed the question, 'How many are Great Britain and Ireland?' Frege was plainly hinting that the question is unanswerable unless one specifies how many *what* are meant; how many sovereign states, how many nations, how many islands. . . .

McTaggart argues that 'three' does not apply to *each* of *A*, *B*, and *C*, so it must apply to them *all together*, as a group. But might we not rather say that taken all together *A*, *B*, and *C* are *one*? Russell was in similar trouble in *Principles of Mathematics* about the 'class as many', corresponding to a list and owning numerical attributes; we have to take *A*, *B*, and *C* together in order that *they* may be said to be three, but we must not take them too much together, or else collectively they will be one! Frege would have been sarcastic about this; he might have said

it was clearly a matter of applying just the right dollop of ontological glue – neither too little, so that the objects fall apart: nor
too much, so that they weld into a unity – and that he himself
had never mastered the technique.

There is indeed no reason to regard a list of names as an expression standing for something *in rebus* as the several names
do. We should rather regard the predicate into which now one
name, now a list of names, can be fitted as an operator that can
take a variable number of operands to form a sentence. Similar
operators are to be found in natural and artificial languages. If
we combine sentences with an *exclusive* 'or' to form a sentence,
we may have two, three, four, etc. component sentences: '*A* or
B', '*A, B,* or *C*', '*A, B, C,* or *D*', etc. And it is easy to see that
though with a non-exclusive 'or' we might take '*A, B, C,* or *D*'
as an abbreviated form of '(*A* or *B*) or (*C* or *D*)', no such reading
is possible with the exclusive 'or'; '(*A* or *B*) or (*C* or *D*)' would
not then come out true precisely when just one of the four components was true, as '*A, B, C,* or *D*' would for the exclusive
reading of 'or'. So here we have a very familiar example of an
operator that can take a variable number of operands. Such
operators are not commonly used in symbolic logic, but Wittgenstein did introduce just such an operator in the *Tractatus*: 'N( )'
would correspond to 'neither . . . nor . . .' in English when the
number of operands was two or more (e.g. 'N(p, q, r)' to 'neither
$p, q,$ nor r'), and this is another operator with a varying number
of operands in the vernacular; with a single argument, 'N( )'
would reduce to plain negation. With this understanding, we
may take '——— alone had a chance to steal the ruby' as an
operator that can form a well-constructed sentence either out of
one name or out of several names. But we need not hold that the
names by themselves, apart from this predicative context into
which they can be fitted, are a syntactically coherent whole;
names by themselves, as Plato said in the *Sophist*, form no *logos*,
no coherent piece of discourse. Thus the problem of what a list
answers to *in rebus* simply disappears.

When we have a list in grammatical subject-position it is
normal, and in some cases clearly correct, to distinguish between
what is predicated *distributively* and what is predicated *collec-*

tively. But here again I do not think we need assume anything *in rebus* except the several substances answering to the several names on the list. There is of course a difference between, '*A, B, C*, are each of them φ' and, '*A, B, C* are all of them together φ'; but to assume different entities (say, with Russell, a class as many and a class as one) for these propositions to be about is extravagant. Russell likewise assumed that different 'combinations' (not effected by any different combining relations) were involved for, '*A, B, C*, are each of them φ' and, 'One of *A, B, C – A* or *B* or *C* – is φ': but we shall probably not feel inclined to follow him here, and if not, neither should we take the difference between collective and distributive predication as corresponding to a difference *in rebus*.

A further complication in McTaggart's theory of groups is his doctrine of repeating groups. There can, he thinks, be groups *of* groups; and then in particular a group may be grouped with members or subgroups of itself; we thus get a repeating group. If we use a semicolon to build up lists whose items are lists, the list '*A, B, C; A, B*' would name a repeating group – so called because in its make-up, McTaggart tells us, the substances *A* and *B* occur twice over (126)! This is pretty obviously nonsense and confusion. The names '*A*' and '*B*' occur twice over; but as Frege said, the object *A* cannot occur twice over, and if you don't believe this, just try occurring twice over yourself! Reverting to the level of language, we may well doubt whether a list with *lists* as items can be coherently constructed, if a list is itself not a syntactically coherent sub-unit in a sentence.

McTaggart's construction of repeating groups was not a gratuitous piece of folly: he had the genuine problem of accounting for the logical form e.g. of a club rule saying that only a certain committee or its sub-committee has authority to do so-and-so. If *A, B, C, D, E* are the members of the committee and *B, D, E* are the members of the sub-committee, must we not accept the sense and possible truth of, 'Only (*A, B, C, D, E*) or (*B, D, E*) have authority to do so-and-so'? and since 'or' in 'Only Tom or Bill had a chance to steal the ruby' forms a list, have we not here 'or' forming a list of two lists (126)?

I shall not even sketch the way one might deal with this

problem; it could not be solved without constructing a full theory of collective predication. But technical difficulties in logic ought not to make us lose our heads in ontology. Whatever complications are needed to bring out the logical structure of the predication, we must not be bamboozled into thinking this predication about the two committees relates to any other substances than just *A, B, C, D,* and *E*. Even groups of these are *entia non grata* if taken as individual substances, and repeating groups of groups ought to be even less welcome.

McTaggart thought he needed the view that a group is a substance in order to get to the notion of a compound substance – a substance that has substances as parts. But we shall see that on the contrary the statement of his theory about compound substances is only embarrassed by the view that each group is a distinct individual substance. In later parts of his work McTaggart quietly drops this view.

McTaggart takes the part-whole relation as primitive; but we may help ourselves here to a device of Nelson Goodman's, and take the overlapping relation as primitive. Either is definable in terms of the other. Let us begin by extending the use of 'part' so that a thing counts as one part of itself; the familiar sense of 'part' can then be expressed by 'proper part', meaning a part other than the whole. Then we may say that *A* and *B* overlap when some *C* is part both of *A* and of *B*; or on the other hand we may say that *A* is a part of *B* when whatever overlaps *A* overlaps *B*. It doesn't matter which relation we take as primitive, but the part of McTaggart's theory we are now coming on to can be stated more neatly in terms of overlapping.

Suppose we have two lists of individual substances, *L* and *L'*, satisfying the condition that a substance *A* overlaps a substance listed in *L* if and only if it overlaps a substance listed in *L'*. (For example, a list of the English counties and a list of the English dioceses would satisfy this condition.) In that case McTaggart says that the two lists correspond to the same content. Whenever there is a definite content, McTaggart thinks, there is an individual substance, and there cannot be two substances with the same content (125). This view, so Broad objects, lands McTaggart in a flat contradiction with what he has said about groups as substances; for the two lists, L, L', will each correspond *in rebus* to a group, which is a distinct individual substance, and yet these two substances *will* have the same content. But the remedy is easy, though Broad does not notice this: McTaggart never ought to have recognized groups as substances, and as I said the recognition is later quietly dropped. McTaggart eased the transition for himself by saying that one and the same substance *is* each of the two groups, if the lists of the groups determine a common content for the substance; this way of speaking is at least not easily defensible (128). But since the idea of a group as an individual substance plays a negligible part in the later development of the theory, the best way to mend McTaggart's exposition is simply to ignore the idea henceforth.

What is important and indispensable in McTaggart's thought is the view that any list of individual substances does determine a content, and thereby specify an individual substance, one overlapped by precisely those substances that overlap the substances on the list; we need not suppose, and cannot consistently suppose, that each new list determines a new substance. A list that includes just the table at which I am now writing, the oldest rabbit in Australia, and the last dose of medicine taken by Louis XV, will determine a certain definite content; it is determinate as regards any other substance whether or not it overlaps with one of these three, and McTaggart holds that there will be some *one* substance A which has the given content, that is to say, which any substance C overlaps if and only if it overlaps one of these three substances. A will be a compound substance with these three substances as parts that together make it up (129). Although we have got rid of many substances by getting rid of groups (particularly the nightmarish hierarchy of repeating groups), the unlimited licence of using any list of substances to specify the content of a new substance still seems a bit exorbitant. But it is worth remarking that other theories about parts and wholes (mereological theories, as Polish logicians would call them) which have been put forward in this century make the same exorbitant assumption: cf. Nelson Goodman's *Structure of Appearance*.

The identity of a compound substance, being given by its

content, depends in McTaggart's opinion solely upon what constituent substances make up the whole; it is quite irrelevant what mutual relations the parts have, to constitute the internal structure of the whole. One and the same set of things may stand simultaneously in different mutual relations: *A*, *B*, *C*, and *D* may be partners in business and may also be the players in a game of bridge on a certain evening, but the same whole, or compound substance, is constituted by *A*, *B*, *C*, and *D* no matter which relations between them we attend to (121, 749). Here again Goodman agrees with McTaggart.

There is a unique substance of maximal content: the Universe. The Universe may be described as that substance which has as a part any substance whatsoever, or of which every other substance is a proper part; or again, in terms of overlapping, we may say that the Universe overlaps every substance. There can be only one substance so characterized: it is easy to prove that any substances satisfying this description will have the same content, whatever overlaps one will overlap another, and so they cannot be distinct substances (135).

What we have shown so far might make us think that (as McTaggart puts it) the Universe has no grain. If we represent the Universe by a circle, any area within the circle, connected or scattered, will represent a substance, and we have thus far no reason to regard any one partition of the Universe into substances as any more important than any other. But this appearance of a grainless Universe will be removed by later developments of the system. As we shall see, McTaggart in fact regards the Universe as differentiated into, and wholly constituted by, a great number of persons; and this way of regarding the make-up of the Universe is for him vastly more important than any other way.

McTaggart has a fundamental principle that *every* substance has content, has proper parts, has an internal structure. (The internal structure comes about because the proper parts are certain to have some definite mutual relations.) None too appropriately, McTaggart sometimes expresses this by saying that every substance is *divisible* or *infinitely divisible*. He has various ways of making this axiom plausible. The kind of simplicity that belongs to indefinable characteristics certainly cannot, he points out, belong to substances. Again, we have no reason in empirical observation or scientific theory to assume absolutely simple and indivisible substances; there are only philosophical arguments in their favour, and these McTaggart would regard as demonstrably fallacious. For example, the arguments about *minima visibilia* or the like in Berkeley and Hume are very grossly confused; and the argument sketched in Wittgenstein's *Tractatus* is one that McTaggart would fault as involving a double use of the word 'complex', now for a compound substance and now for a fact about substances (we have already gone into this in Chapter 2).

Further, McTaggart would maintain, with some justification, that some philosophers who have claimed to believe in simple substances have not really meant what they said. For example, Leibniz calls his monads simple; but on the other hand he holds that every monad mirrors within it all other monads, and this would imply an *infinitely* complicated internal structure for each monad (as will be obvious when we consider McTaggart's similar theory of Determining Correspondence).

One particular argument of McTaggart's in this area deserves special consideration. It is designed to show, not that no substances are in fact simple, but that we have no reason to think any substances in our experience are simple. If a substance lasts a finite time, it has temporal parts, McTaggart argues: thus, take my cat Batty; since different things can be predicated of Batty at time t_1 and t_2, Batty at t_1 is a different individual substance from Batty at t_2. So any familiar object of experience is not given as a simple substance, but rather, as differentiated into successive temporal stages. Even if time is unreal, as McTaggart is going to argue, this apparent differentiation will correspond to a real though non-temporal array of distinct parts (163–6).

I find this notion of temporal parts extremely suspect; and it is worth while to go into the matter, because it is not just old history. The idea that a concrete object like a cat has successive temporal parts is put forward e.g. by Quine in *Word and Object*. Quine appears not to have noticed the difficulty about parsing, 'Batty caught a mouse at t_1' as, '(Batty at t_1) caught a mouse';

namely, that it is by no means clear that mouse-catching can be ascribed to a temporal past of a cat rather than to a cat. (Not to speak of the fact that we'd need to speak of a mouse-at-t_1, e.g. M-at-t_1 for some mouse M, as what was caught – and can the catcher–caught relation really hold between Batty-at-t_1 and M-at-t_1?) The advocates of temporal parts might at this point ask for leave to vary their plea. When temporal parts are introduced, they must have new predicates, not the familiar ordinary-language predicates. But the court ought to refuse leave to vary the plea. The original ground for distinguishing the substances Batty-at-t_1 and Batty-at-t_2 within Batty was that e.g. Batty caught a mouse at t_1 but not at t_2, and this was parsed as an ascription of mouse-catching to Batty-at-t_1 but not to Batty-at-t_2. But if the characteristic that is to be ascribed to Batty-at-t_1 but denied to Batty-at-t_2 is *not* mouse-catching after all but some other characteristic, the theorist of temporal parts has really been sawing away at the branch he is sitting on: for the ground for distinguishing the alleged parts of Batty, Batty-at-t_1, and Batty-at-t_2, was precisely that we thought we *had hold* of characteristics that one had and the other lacked.

The idea of temporal parts seems to apply to events or processes, not to enduring bodies like Batty; people who have believed in temporal parts have accordingly often sought to rub out this distinction between processes and things, or occurrents and continuants, and have used such language as 'long events' for cats and cabbages and kings. It is not surprising that McTaggart ignores the distinction; for there is no direct way of maintaining it if, as McTaggart thinks, time is a delusion, nor is there any simple construction of an analogous notion that would still apply even if time is a delusion.

With regard to McTaggart's axiom that whatever is a substance has parts, complexity, internal structure, I have here no more to remark except that McTaggart unquestioningly assumes that the notion of parts and whole, and other related notions like complexity, internal structure, content, are univocal, and that this upon consideration appears extremely doubtful. One application he has is to mental events as parts of the person; another, as we have just seen, is the application to temporal parts, or what corresponds to them in reality if there is no time; a third is to spatial parts of spatial wholes. We may be doubtful whether there is more than an analogy here; it is useful to compare Wittgenstein's illustrations of different sorts of composition in the *Philosophical Investigations*. Wittgenstein was using these illustrations to cast doubt on his own thesis in the *Tractatus* that substance is composed of simple individuals; but they would equally serve to make us doubt McTaggart's 'self-evident' theses about wholes and parts. Here I must content myself with registering the doubt.

A bit of McTaggart's vocabulary concerning parts and wholes should here be specially noted; it will be frequently used in the sequel. Besides saying that *A* has *B*, *C*, *D*, as parts, he will say that *A* is differentiated into *B*, *C*, and *D*; he uses the noun 'differentiation' both for the parts *B*, *C*, and *D* themselves and for the fact or characteristic of being differentiated (I do not think this possible ambiguity ever fails to get resolved by the context). Sometimes this phraseology gives McTaggart's thought a less harsh or awkward expression: e.g. to say that a person is differentiated in respect of his mental states is less harsh than saying his mental states are parts of him. But we must always remember that the change is only a verbal one, and that for McTaggart there is no doubt that the relation of part and whole is one that can be univocally signified in what may seem very heterogeneous examples.

6 Matter and sense-data

Let us summarize our results thus far. All substances other than the Universe are parts of the Universe; and all substances have parts that are themselves substances, and thus have parts within parts to infinity; moreover, any set of substances can be taken together as having content which is the content of some one single substance. The Universe can thus be sliced into parts in an infinity of different ways; and thus far we have no reason to regard one partition of the Universe as more important than another. Thus far, the Universe seems to have no grain. Each substance has indeed a sufficient description, in terms of merely general characteristics, and all its characteristics admit of completely accurate specification, according to what I have called the principle of ontological determinacy. But thus far it is as though we had a vast collection of books with no duplicates, but had no idea of how they might be ordered and catalogued.

McTaggart is going to argue that the abstract principles we have studied have a most devastating consequence: he offers to prove that materiality is a delusive characteristic, that nothing real is material, that nothing possesses extension or colour or any of the ostensible attributes of bodies, that there are not even individuals (like the philosophers' sense-data) which have some but not all of the attributes commonly regarded as special to material bodies. The whole show of the material world is for McTaggart a veil of Maya disguising the reality.

This conclusion is just as paradoxical as McTaggart's well-known denial of the reality of time, and I think it deserves the same serious consideration as has in fact been given to the other argument. Of course I am not seriously apprehensive lest McTaggart may turn out to have proved his point; lest perhaps (as Yeats, who had read McTaggart, put it):

this pragmatical, preposterous pig of a world, its farrow that
so solid seem,
Must vanish on the instant if the mind but change its theme.

But I do think that McTaggart, like Zeno arguing against the
reality of motion, has produced an immensely interesting and
significant argument; and when once philosophers start considering McTaggart's argument against matter seriously, we
shall get the same situation as we have for Zeno's arguments and
for McTaggart's own argument about time. There will be general
agreement that the conclusion is false, but little agreement about
what is wrong with the argument.

I think the reason is plain why this important argument has
been neglected. In his style of presentation, as opposed to the
substance of the argument, McTaggart committed two serious
mistakes. We may call these the *tactical* and the *strategic* mistake.
The tactical mistake arose from McTaggart's late adoption of a
view of sense-perception which was not organically connected
with any important ideas of his; it could be completely eliminated
from his work by making a few cuts and consequential changes.
The strategic mistake arose from a firmly held, but to my mind
quite wrong-headed, attitude of McTaggart's about method in
metaphysics. I shall argue that correction of this mistake would
leave us with a system having the same main outlines and conclusions as McTaggart's; but drastic changes within the edifice
would be needed, and McTaggart might well have regarded such
changes as inadmissible. Even here, though, we must remember
that McTaggart originally planned a *Dialectic of Existence* in
Hegelian style, and then recast his work in a more accessible
style of argument; so reconstruction of the same main lines of
thought with a radical change of method is something to which
McTaggart might himself have resorted as a defensive measure.

McTaggart's tactical mistake was to introduce into his system
the notion of sense-data or sensa. Most of McTaggart's Cambridge contemporaries – who thought of themselves, as Moore's
Some Main Problems of Philosophy amusingly reveals, as 'the
overwhelming majority of philosophers'! – accepted this doctrine
of sensa as not only true but plainly true: anyone who then
thought otherwise, or had previously thought otherwise, or

should thereafter think otherwise, must be just muddle-headed. I learned something of that Cambridge milieu from long conversations with my father, who was an undergraduate a few years before the First World War. McTaggart had clearly not accepted the sense-datum theory before the war; for during the war he reissued *Some Dogmas of Religion* 60–111 as a small book to comfort the bereaved, and by implication this book rejects the theory. He unwisely accepted the current Cambridge doctrine a short time later, when he was writing *The Nature of Existence*. But it is easy to show that this doctrine is not coherently placeable within the framework of McTaggart's system.

Sense-datum theorists hold that sense-data *really* have those characteristics which the material objects perceived by sense *appear* to have (or at least that sense-data have *some* of these characteristics – the principle of selection is not altogether clear). For example, the object I call a penny *appears*, to my sense of sight at a given moment, as brown and elliptical; the perceptual situation would involve a sense-datum that *really is* brown and elliptical. Since the distinction between sensible appearance and the real attributes of bodies is just what sense-data were introduced to explain, there must be no such distinction, between the way they appear and the way they are, for sense-data themselves; they just are what they sensibly appear to be. And so our cognitive relation to material things like pennies must be different from our cognitive relation to sense-data of these bodies: sense-data would be presented (or sensed, or prehended, or whatever) just as they are, with no room for error; whereas the perceptual acceptance (to use one of the terms that were invented) of there being a *body* with such-and-such attributes would be fallible.

I do not think this theory can be brusquely dismissed. Its holders were sometimes excessively self-confident, but they were hard-working philosophers who tried strenuously to be clear, and they knew what an argument was. Sooner any day ten pages from one of the better sense-datum theorists than the endless natterings about the correct English usage of the verbs 'look', 'seem', and 'appear'! But whatever its intrinsic merits, the sense-datum theory is irreconcilable with McTaggart's thought. There are two decisive reasons for saying this.

First, as I said, the characteristics ascribed to sense-data are just a selection from those which unphilosophical talk ascribes to bits of matter. There are indeed certain differences: the criterion for persistent identity through time would be different for a body and for a sense-datum; again, it would be held that a sense-datum, unlike a body, could not combine such qualities as colour, flavour, and hardness. But McTaggart's claim is that we cannot without contradiction ascribe to *any* substance *only* the commonly recognized characteristics of matter; and this conclusion would *a fortiori* imply that no real individual can have *only* the characteristics that philosophers ascribe to sense-data, since these are just a selection from the ones commonly ascribed to matter. Naturally, McTaggart saw this (376–8).

McTaggart's next step after refuting the reality of matter will be to show that on a certain hypothesis – the hypothesis of 'determining correspondence' – persons and their mental states can exist without our running into the contradiction that was fatal to matter; but that the characteristics of persons and their states are incompatible with those commonly ascribed to matter. Now clearly this argument tells against a double-aspect theory regardless of whether an individual is regarded as combining a personal and a material aspect, or as being (say) under one aspect a state of mind and under the other a red square sense-datum. And again McTaggart notices this (429–31).

But then the occupation of sense-data is gone. Sense-data were to be individuals *really* possessing the characteristics that bodies *appear* to have. But if all that really exists is spiritual individuals misperceived as having these bodily characteristics, it is a wholly futile complication to say we misperceive these individuals as *sense-data*; much better drop all talk of sense-data, and say we misperceive some spiritual individuals as *bodies* with certain sensible characteristics. McTaggart in fact very often does drop sense-datum language and talk in just this way (e.g. in 368).

In the second place, it was integral to the sense-datum theory that sense-data should be cognized otherwise and more directly than the bodies whose sense-data they were. But we shall see later that on McTaggart's view there *are* no such different species of cognition. Any appearance that there are different species, more or less direct sorts of cognition, is itself an introspective misperception of what goes on in our minds (426). So McTaggart cannot consistently hold that in seeing a penny I merely 'perceptually accept' it as a solid body, but 'prehend' a brown elliptical sensum. For McTaggart, perception – which may well be misperception – is the only form of cognition that actually occurs; in 'seeing a penny' what I am doing is to (mis)perceive some individual as being *both* a solid body *and* brown and elliptical; and again this way of speaking, which alone is consistent on his part, is one that he frequently drops into, forgetting about sensa.

I conclude that all reference to sensa on McTaggart's system is an alien growth that should be ruthlessly and fearlessly excised. Such excision would often manifestly make McTaggart's argument clearer and more convincing; let the reader just try his hand e.g. at rewriting 413 in terms of perceiving a *carpet*, instead of *a sensum of* a carpet! I shall henceforth discuss McTaggart as if thus rewritten throughout, and say no more about sensa.

Broad's commentary also takes the liberty of rewriting McTaggart's text; instead of eliminating talk about sensa, he accepts it, but alters McTaggart's 'perceive' and 'perception' to 'prehend' and 'prehension'. This cannot but falsify McTaggart's thought. 'Prehension' was a Cambridge philosophers' term of art for the supposed special cognitive relation of a mind to sense-data; for McTaggart there are no species of cognitive relation and there are no sense-data. We shall see that at a later crucial point Broad's way of treating *The Nature of Existence* as though McTaggart had written 'prehension' and not 'perception' leads to a total breakdown of understanding.

Now for McTaggart's strategic error. Hitherto I have not found it necessary to bring Hegel into the exposition of McTaggart's philosophy; but at this point I must discuss, not indeed what the right interpretation of Hegel is (that would be impossible to attempt here) but how McTaggart read his Hegel and what general ideas of philosophical method he derived from Hegel as he read him. McTaggart thought that you could derive *a priori* a highly complicated scheme of abstract categories without bringing in the familiar concrete characteristics of things except as mere illustrations needed psychologically. And the right method of philosophy was to begin by deducing the category-structure of the existent in great detail and then to see which apparent characteristics of the existent conform to the categorial scheme thus laid down *a priori*.

Up to the point we just reached, nothing that McTaggart has deduced, not even the infinite differentiation of substance (of itself and without further inference), is incompatible with ordinary experience and our ordinary view of the world. But McTaggart thought that you could develop an abstract categorial scheme further, and that then you would get categories which could only be exemplified in *some* of the descriptions that seem to be empirically grounded, and not in other of these descriptions; and then the descriptions that would fit these abstract categories could be accepted as possibly correct and the empirical descriptions that would not fit these abstract categories could be dismissed as delusive.

I think that this whole idea of philosophical method, metaphysical method, was a mistake. Anyhow, it leads to McTaggart's presenting his argument much more obscurely and much more vulnerably than he would have done if he had not had this general idea of metaphysical method. However, I emphasize again that this idea of metaphysical method was very deeply ingrained. Cutting out sense-data, which McTaggart had come to talk about only five or six years before he wrote *The Nature of Existence*, makes only a trivial change; the other change that I am making in the presentation of his system is a big change. His major philosophical work before he got on to writing of his own nature of existence was a very detailed commentary on Hegel's Logic; in this he traced Hegel's attempted deduction of an abstract category-scheme, to which any empirical content that is not delusive must conform; and at the end of the book he said that after decades of work on Hegel, he thought that Hegel had penetrated deeper into the nature of reality than any other philosopher. So deep-rooted was this conviction of McTaggart's that the right way to do things was to construct this abstract category-scheme first and then see what would fit into it.

However, I do not propose to follow McTaggart's order of exposition, but a different order. The chapter 'The Contradiction of Infinite Divisibility' (XXIII) purports to show that except on a certain condition infinite divisibility is a self-contradictory notion; this is a very abstract and entangled piece of argument, and is practically incomprehensible unless you see what it is in aid of, and study it in connection with the argumentation in concrete material that it is leading up to (chapter XXXIV in vol. 2), namely, argumentation about the unreality of matter. The next chapter following upon this, 'Determining Correspondence' (XXIV), is, I think, even more difficult to understand; we need to consider it in conjunction with the chapter called 'Cogitation' (XXXVII in the second volume of *The Nature of Existence*), where McTaggart considers what he takes to be the only actual embodiment of this abstract category of determining correspondence.

I shall now state the argument about the unreality of matter. This argument, as I say, would be designed to prove also that any individuals which have only those characteristics, or those kinds of characteristics, which are commonly ascribed to material things, must be delusory. It is not tied to a particular view about, say, primary and secondary qualities. So if one wants to consider how McTaggart is related to Berkeley, there is a very striking difference between them. Berkeley thought that there were things whose existence consisted in being perceived; McTaggart quite clearly thought that such a notion was an incoherent one, that a thing's actual existence is logically prior to the perception of the thing. Berkeley thought that the qualities of what he called 'ideas' were correctly perceived, that things really are red, and hot, and so on, and that there is no delusion in the case at all; whereas McTaggart thought that the individual things perceived were real and independent, but practically all our perception of them was delusory – must be delusory, because an ascription to sense-objects of the characteristics that are vulgarly ascribed to them leads, one way or another, to a flat inconsistency.

We need to consider two sorts of characteristics of matter (or of matter-like individuals, such as Berkeley's ideas or the Cambridge philosophers' sense-data would be): on the one hand, spatial characteristics – shape, size, spatial relations and so on; and on the other hand what I shall call 'extensible qualities' – qualities that are spread out over the individuals that they characterize. (The phrase 'spread out' is one that you get, e.g. in Moore's *Some Main Problems of Philosophy* – he says that whiteness is *spread out over* the white thing.) McTaggart claims that a body which has *only*, on the one hand, spatial characteristics, and on the other hand, extensible characteristics is an impossibility, because the existence of such an individual is incompatible with the principles of sufficient description, ontological determinacy (in his own jargon, 'total ultimate presupposition' – but we can forget that), and complete differentiation into parts of parts of parts *ad infinitum*.

It is of course not of itself paradoxical to say that what is extended is divided into parts of parts *ad infinitum*. Geometry is much easier if you assume that lines and so on can be divided *ad infinitum* than if you assume that you come down to minimal bits of extension which cannot be subdivided. Berkeley and Hume, who were bad mathematicians, suppose that you would only have to pare off some of the more refined parts of geometry, like that nasty new-fangled calculus, if you assumed that space was divisible into a finite number of indivisible parts. They were, however, grossly wrong.

It is the other two principles, combined with the principle of infinite differentiation that give rise to our trouble: in particular, the principle that I have already talked about, the principle of ontological determinacy. Let me give a bird's eye view of the argument. Any bit of matter or quasi-matter (henceforth, for simplicity, I shall just say 'matter') will have parts within parts *ad infinitum*; and by the principle of sufficient description, each of these parts will have to have a description in completely general terms, characterizing it alone. But then, we run into difficulties with the third principle, the principle of ontological determinacy; for we get an unending series of more and more specific descriptions of the internal structure of matter, and this series will neither have a limit nor a last term; this is something that is excluded by the principle of ontological determinacy. I mean: however fine a division of the bits of matter into parts you consider, there will be a division into tinier parts, which themselves will have descriptions characterizing them and differentiating them from one another. This will be a more detailed, more specific description of the internal structure of the bodies first considered. And so on *ad infinitum*: we get an infinite series of more and more specific descriptions, but never a *most* specific or *most* determinate description. This is what is excluded by the principle of complete ontological determinacy. And therefore if the three principles used here as premises – sufficient description, ontological determinacy, and complete differentiation *ad infinitum* – are all true, then matter cannot exist. This is a bird's eye view of the argument; I now go into more detail.

First let us discuss non-geometrical qualities, extensible qualities, like colour, or density, or temperature, or electric charge or the like. Here we get a number of different possibilities. We may suppose that at a certain stage of division, a body is homogeneous with regard to non-geometrical qualities – with regard to extensible qualities. In that case, unless we can specify the geometrical qualities as well, we already have a difficulty, because we no longer have the possibility of describing the more minute divisions of the body, although we know that there must be such. We might suppose that there was a sort of lawless series of qualities which just happened to come along: e.g. that a body was divisible up to a certain stage into differently *coloured* parts, and beyond that stage into differently *tasting* parts, and so on, with a new species of quality at each stage to differentiate the parts. But it is a rather wild supposition that the differentiation of bodies *ad infinitum* is carried out by having an infinite number of genera of extensible qualities (356).

We might try sticking to one genus of extensible quality and suppose that at no stage of division is a body homogeneous; let us say that it has a really continuous variation of colour, and that however small a bit of the body we take, one half of that bit is differently coloured from the other half. In that case, however far down the series one went, one would be able to discriminate the two halves from one another by descriptions relating to their colour. (The continuously varying quality need not of course be colour; it could be the intensity of an electromagnetic field, or something like that.)

This suggestion, however natural, is excluded by the principle of complete ontological determinacy. Although you could, for an arbitrary number of stages of sub-division, distinguish the parts of a body in respect of this supposed continuously varying quality, but then you would have the situation, excluded by this principle, that there would be a series of more and more complete specifications which does not terminate in a limit or last term, in a most complete specification – does not so terminate even in principle. For *ex hypothesi*, we can ascribe no completely determinate form of this determinable extensible characteristic to any bit of matter as a whole; and we get a more specific determination if the one half and the other half of a body are further specified in respect of colour, let us say. This series could terminate only if it were possible, in the limit, to ascribe colour, or some other extensible characteristic, to a mere point; and for McTaggart of course, this is impossible. Extensible characteristics, for one thing, cannot belong to points but only to extended objects; and for another thing, there are no points to ascribe such a characteristic to (356).

However, it might very well seem that we could determine parts within parts, to infinity, by very simple geometrical constructions; e.g. any cube consists of eight cubes each again consists of eight cubes, and so on *ad infinitum* and that therefore, even if at a certain stage of division we got to a thing that was completely homogeneous in respect of the extensible or non-spatial characteristics that are commonly ascribed to matter, all the same, it could be differentiated *ad infinitum* by some such construction as this, by considering its geometrical characteristics. McTaggart thought that this was not so, and that our temptation to think otherwise depended upon false imagination.

We identify bits of an extended thing, McTaggart says, in two ways. In the first place, we identify each bit by considering some extensible quality that characterizes a certain region as a whole: 'Thus we can discriminate a particular surface by the fact that all its parts are blue while everything which touches it is red. It is also the case, when we mark off a section of a homogeneous blue line by measuring it against a non-graduated stick, for then every part of that section has the quality of being in contact with that stick. And the stick is discriminated by the fact that every part of it has qualities, in respect of colour and hardness, which are not possessed by anything in contact with it' (360).

That is one way; but this only discriminates a whole from what surrounds it. This is clearly no way to discriminate parts within parts *ad infinitum*.

The second way is that each part is discriminated by saying which sub-parts it itself consists of; we can identify certain sub-parts, and then we can identify the whole as the whole which consists of those sub-parts. But this obviously is not a method that could be applied to parts within parts to infinity; that the individuation of a whole should depend on the individuation of its parts, and that on the individuation of their parts, and so on, *ad infinitum*. This would be a vicious sort of regress, as McTaggart says; and he considers that we only believe that geometrical considerations such that I have sketched to you could identify parts within parts to infinity, because we have at the back of our minds the second sort of identification – identifying parts of a body by the things that are in turn *their* parts; let us say identifying those parts of a map of Great Britain which together constitute the map of England, by picking out, by their different colours, all the different counties of England, and then saying that the England part of the map is the part consisting of all these various county parts. We cannot apply this to parts within parts *ad infinitum*.

Let us however fix our minds firmly on the idea of a qualitatively homogeneous extended bit of something: if it is qualitatively homogeneous, then it just has not got actual parts at all, let alone parts of parts *ad infinitum*. This last dictum, which McTaggart assumes to be true, is again, like many of his dicta, not one peculiar to him. You will find in Hume the same notion of something extended which is homogeneous in every qualitative respect, in respect of every extensible quality, and which thus cannot have actual parts. You get the same idea in the medieval Scholastics; the company is rather a strange one, but that is not my fault!

The solutions found by the other holders of this premise would be unacceptable to McTaggart. The medieval solution was to say that when you have a completely homogeneous continuum there are not any actual parts, but only potential parts. (In their ignorance of physics, they were more ready to think they had come upon instances of a completely homogeneous continuum than we should be; but that, I think, is not relevant.) Though as a matter of history McTaggart had a great respect for Aquinas, he certainly was not going to buy this idea; for reasons which ought to be apparent from what I said earlier, he would regard the conception of real potentiality as a thoroughly mirky and messy one. Potentiality, for him, is a conception partly due to muddled and untenable ideas regarding what corresponds *in rebus* to counterfactual conditionals. Partly, again, our idea of possibility relates to what McTaggart called *intrinsic* determination; that is, if it is not the case that being *A* intrinsically determines *not* being *B*, then *being A and B* is possible. This idea of a possibility, as the absence of a certain intrinsic determination between characteristics, would in McTaggart's eyes be sound; but it plainly is not going to help to make sense of the notion of potential parts. Hume's idea of solving the problems of infinite divisibility, by saying that at a certain stage divisibility just stops, would get even shorter shrift from McTaggart.

So McTaggart concludes that you cannot regard matter as having any possibility of sufficient description of its parts within parts *ad infinitum* which yet conforms to the principle of onto-logical determinateness: whether you consider extensible characteristics alone, or consider geometrical characteristics as well. He considers the question whether bringing in Time as a dimension would make things any better. Roughly speaking, his answer is: In the first place, there is not such a thing as Time; but we need not make a fuss about that, because one might very well hold that there was a real dimension of matter which was misperceived as being Time. (And this in fact, though not in express words, is the view held by certain sorts of so-called scientific realists; what J. J. C. Smart's 'scientific realism', let us say, really amounts to, though Smart would not want to put it that way, is the doctrine that there is not really any time or change, but there is a dimension of matter which is misperceived as time.) Supposing that this were so, then the arguments that go over for space and geometrical characteristics, go over *mutatis mutandis* with reference to this supposed dimension, and therefore do not avail to save or defend the reality of matter.

There is just one last chance for real things to have material characteristics; viz. that what has matterlike characteristics might also have, though this was not patent, certain other characteristics. We might suppose that though things were not divisible *ad infinitum* in their material dimensions, the materially simple parts of things had an internal structure in some other, non-material, dimension. McTaggart says that this, though an abstract possibility, is something that we have every reason to dismiss. For we shall see that the three principles, which McTaggart says matter cannot satisfy, can on a certain hypothesis be satisfied by spiritual reality. We know that there is spiritual reality: we know that there are persons with mental states, though the characteristics vulgarly ascribed to persons are very different from the characteristics they would have to have in order to satisfy McTaggart's principles. On the other hand, McTaggart thinks he can prove that persons and their states cannot have any material or matter-like characteristics; and so the only things given in our experience which on a suitable hypothesis could satisfy McTaggart's principles are such as *could not* have any material characteristics. And things that have *only* material characteristics are impossible anyhow. McTaggart's general conclusion is that it is utterly unfounded to believe that anything is matter, or that anything has any material characteristic. Matter, as he loved to say, is in the same position as the Gorgons and the Harpies.

Additional note

I have left Chapter 6 as I wrote it originally. I have added the present note since reading the Trinity College MS – comprising

Draft A and McTaggart's notes towards preparing Draft B.

My remarks about the alienness to McTaggart's system of the sense-datum theory, and about the botched work by which he tried to incorporate it, are fully borne out by Draft A. I mentioned the greater naturalness of 413 if rewritten in terms of perceiving (certain substances as) a carpet and its parts; Draft A in fact does speak simply of 'perceptions of the whole and of the parts' – the words 'of the datum perceived in such an experience' were added in later drafts. Similarly, in 597, when discussing confused perception, McTaggart follows Leibniz in using the example of perceiving the sound of the sea falling on the beach. In the published Draft B McTaggart apologizes for this example, on the score that on the 'ordinary' view (this is no doubt the same view as Moore tells us is held by 'the overwhelming majority of philosophers'!) this is not a matter of misperception but of 'difference of the percepta caused by the waves to hearers at different distances'. In Draft A however McTaggart makes no apology for this example, and in fact writes as follows:

A half-mile inland I perceive clearly, so that I can recognize it, the sound of the sea falling on the beaches. I have no perceptions of the single waves which are sufficiently clear for me to recognize them. But the qualities which I recognize by perception in the sound of the sea are largely determined by the perceptions of the individual waves, which are below the level of consciousness.

We may notice that there is no reference here to sense-data as objects of perception.

Though nearly all the changes from Draft A (apart from the ones bringing in sense-data) are decided improvements, and very little in vol. 2 betrays that the work as we read it is the result of an editor's handling imperfectly revised MSS, chapter XXXIV is an exception: the printed text gives the impression of unfinished work inadequately presented. Nobody who has experienced the difficulty of editing a *Nachlass* for the press will judge Broad harshly for not doing the best possible job on the material he was editing: though someone who had more sympathy with McTaggart's enterprise might have done better. The text actually published made it necessary for me, at more than one place, to guess what the intended course of the argument was, without much direct textual support. It is gratifying that my divination of McTaggart's thought is borne out by the Trinity MSS.

The reason for rejecting the suggestion that a body could have a really continuous variation of colour, so that however far down one went in the series of parts within parts one would be able to discriminate parts from each other by colour-descriptions, is not stated in the printed text in the form I have given it in this commentary. But precisely that ground for rejection *is* to be found in the Trinity MS – in a note giving the changes to be made in preparing Draft B from Draft A:

> If the primary part were blue, its parts couldn't be other colours. You couldn't avoid this by saying that it could be blue modified by yellow, red, etc. For then no part of it would be the blue which was modified – let alone the whole of it being so. Nor could it have the quality of being some sort of blue, the parts being each some definite shade of blue. For anything which is coloured at all must have some precise colour; and on this view nothing would have precise colour until we reached the end of an infinite series.

The suggestion that parts within parts to infinity might be determined by the eight-fold division (say) of a qualitatively homogeneous cube into eight cubes is a very natural one: I had forgotten that Broad makes it in his *Examination*, vol. 2, pp. 245ff., but on re-reading Broad's over-elaborate discussion I am surprised that he thinks he has answered *ambulando* all objections that McTaggart has raised or might raise. This very construction is in fact already mentioned by McTaggart in Draft A; and he naturally did not think the suggestion renders matter impregnable to his objections.

It is not clear in the printed text of chapter XXXIV that McTaggart did explicitly hold the view I alleged to be his ground for rejecting this sort of suggestion – namely, the view, shared by him with Hume and the medieval Scholastics, that what is extended and qualitatively homogeneous in all respects cannot have parts, not *actual* parts. The nearest we come to a statement of this view is at the top of p. 39 in vol. 2. However, in the notes

McTaggart made for preparing Draft B, we find the explicit words:

And then what would separate each part from the next, so as to be able to say, *this* has this shape and size? Nothing, if they were otherwise homogeneous.

7 Time

The information some philosophers have about McTaggart's philosophy is like what the laconic President Calvin Coolidge volunteered about the sermon: 'It was about Time' (rather than Sin), 'and he was agin it.' Those who know a bit more than that often concentrate wholly upon his argument for the unreality of time. He does not deserve that this argument should be the only thing in his philosophy to be remembered; but it clearly is one of the greatest of philosophical arguments, as the large number of mutually inconsistent refutations ought to show.

Wonderment about time is one of the perennial sources of genuine philosophy; it comes about from the human condition; we may recollect those two working men whom I heard arguing about time in a Leeds pub. If G. E. Moore is to be believed, he never felt such wonderment about the world, but only about what other philosophers said about the world, for example what McTaggart said about time. I hope Moore did himself an injustice; for his self-description closely corresponds to what Schopenhauer gives as the mark of the bogus philosopher: one who gets his puzzles out of a book and not out of the world.

An unfortunate, though only superficial, aspect of McTaggart's writing on time is his referring to a number of different series, alphabetically labelled: the *A*, *B*, *C*, and *D* series. The *B* series is simply the order of events as earlier and later. This series cannot exist, as described, if there is no time; but it would still on that supposition be possible that what we misperceive as a series of events in time really is a series, though not a series of events, and that whenever we seem to perceive an event *X* occurring in between events *W* and *Y*, these are real individuals, really forming a series, and the place of *X* in that series really is in between *W* and *Y*, though the ordering relations of the series are non-temporal. McTaggart believed that this is indeed so, and he called this supposed real serial order the C series.

Events are also said to form an A series, in respect of being past, present, or future: but as McTaggart presents this idea it is not at all clear why he speaks of a *series*, or what is supposed to be the ordering relation of the series. Happily we need not dwell on this. For we may follow McTaggart in distinguishing two kinds of *prima facie* existent characteristics, both required if there is time: A-characteristics and B-characteristics. A-characteristics are characteristics like being present, being past, being future, being yesterday, being ten years ago, etc.: they can be ascribed only from some standpoint taken as present. B-characteristics are characteristics like being earlier or later than some event, lasting an hour, being ten years apart in birthdays, etc.: on the face of it these involve no relation to a particular present. If we wished to transpose all this to a linguistic key, we might speak rather of A-expressions and B-expressions in our temporal language; but such transposition would be very alien to McTaggart, and, as we have seen in other cases, need not bring us to a better understanding of the points at issue.

The outline of McTaggart's argument is easily stated; the real work is to understand the various steps.

There is no time if there is no change.

There is no change unless A-characteristics actually occur in the world.

But to assume the actual occurrence of A-characteristics involves contradiction.

Ergo: There is no change and no time; whatever individuals there are exist eternally.

I shall not argue about the first premise, which few people would deny; but we need to consider an important puzzle about the term 'change'. McTaggart asserts that if anything changes then everything changes. This paradoxical thesis is easily shown to be true, if we understand the verb 'change' as applying to what I have called *Cambridge* changes. An object O is said to 'change' in this sense if and only if there are two propositions about O, differing only in that one mentions an earlier and the other a later time, and one is true, the other false. I call this an account of 'Cambridge' change, because it was nowise peculiar to McTaggart, but the common property of the Cambridge philosophers at that time: see e.g. Russell's *Principles of Mathematics*, S 442. To avoid all possible misunderstanding, let me emphasize that in using this term I intend no aspersion against this piece of Cambridge philosophy, nor do I deny that this aspect is an integral aspect of change. Whenever there is a Cambridge change, there has been real change somewhere: at least the time will have run on, and that involves change. Conversely, whenever an object O has changed it will satisfy the condition for the occurrence of a Cambridge change. Cambridge change, which alone is considered by McTaggart, is essential to the being of change, and without it there could be no change.

Given this notion of change, it is simply true that if anything changes everything changes. However immutable God may be in his own mind and nature, if some man's relation to God is different at different times, there has been a Cambridge change concerning God. And even if numbers are supposed to be timeless objects, they too will be subject to Cambridge change, for '2 is the number of NN's children at time t' may be true and, '2 is the number of NN's children at time t'' false. Moreover, past events will change, and if things can pass out of existence they will undergo Cambridge change after they have perished. Even if Socrates completely perished at death, he undergoes a Cambridge change if a fresh schoolboy comes to admire him, and even though the killing of Caesar by Brutus was long past, it underwent a Cambridge change when it inspired the French revolutionaries in the 1790s.

Protests against these conclusions would to my mind just be misunderstandings; the Cambridge conception of change is a clear one, and these are its consequences. Moreover, it is the only clear, sharp, conception of change we have. But we may rightly accept notions that we cannot as yet bring into sharp mental focus. We certainly seem to have another conception of a change: a conception, as we may say, of an *actual* change. By this conception, God would not be said to undergo actual change if he does not pass from one state of mind to another; the actual change, if a man has now this, now that, attitude towards God, would lie solely on the man's side. If Theaetetus grows and becomes taller than Socrates, Socrates has *eo ipso* undergone a Cambridge change, since Socrates was taller than Theaetetus at time *t'* but not at time *t*; but it was Theaetetus who *actually* changed. And no past event, no person or thing that has perished, can undergo any actual change at all; still less can numbers do so.

I do not know how to explicate further the conception of actual change. Any object that undergoes actual change is subject to Cambridge change; and if there were no actual change of anything there would be no Cambridge change, and that means: no change at all. But it seems clear that not every subject of Cambridge change thereby undergoes actual change. What undergoes actual change has distinct phases in its history: a long-past event like the killing of Caesar has not a series of stages in its history occurring later on, nor has anything that really has perished a posthumous development from one state to another; God has no history if his mind and will do not change, and it would be raving nonsense to consider the history of a number. Yet past events and perished things, and God, and even numbers, are subject to Cambridge changes.

I cannot develop this line of thought; but it is worth remarking that McTaggart's philosophy, which denies change, could point to a difference in reality underlying the apparent difference between actual change and *merely* Cambridge change. According to McTaggart, when we perceive an object as having diverse stages in its history and thereby undergoing an actual change, this means that the object has a complex internal structure: its parts are ordered in a real non-temporal order, a *C* series, and it is this non-temporal array of parts that we misperceive as a temporal series of stages in the object's history. The striking apparent characteristic of actual change, as opposed to *merely* Cambridge change, would thus answer to a genuine characteristic of the object we are misperceiving: to use a phrase McTaggart borrows from Leibniz, it is a *phaenomenon bene fundatum*.

For his second premise, that change involves *A*-character-istics, McTaggart has three distinct arguments.

His first reason is, I think, very bad indeed. He argues that there is no change unless *events* change, and change in one particular way: from being future through being present to being past. Not only would concrete things have events as phases in their history: each event in such a history would itself have a history, whose phases were the event's futurity, its presentness, and its pastness (311). It does not take very much philosophical nose or *nous* to find in this an idle bandying of words.

If indeed the transitions of ordinary events from futurity to presentness and then to pastness were themselves events, second-order events, our inference could not legitimately stop here; we should have to regard the corresponding things 'happening to' second-order events, *their* becoming present and then becoming past, as third-order events – and so on to infinity. And we should correspondingly get an infinity of times – time 1, time 2, ... A thinker once popular, J. W. Dunne, thought he had *discovered* the existence of all these time-dimensions; many people found the philosophy of Dunne inspiring, for it offered proofs of human freedom and immortality and of God. (Its appeal was also due in part to an occultistic element; Dunne held that in dreams our mind lives in time 2 rather than in time 1, and can thus survey events that in time 1 are still future.)

Dunne thought he had discovered time-dimensions of the real world; McTaggart on the contrary was using the same verbal manipulations to prove the non-existence of time. Both, I think, were bemused by features of our language. But not everybody has seen what the right prophylaxis is against this befuddling influence. Against McTaggart and Dunne people have often argued that 'past', 'present', and 'future' are not proper predicates; the 'change' of an event from being future through being present to being past is not logically assimilable to the change e.g. of colours in a bruise. But what in general has been ignored is that you cannot cast doubt on the logical status of a term as a predicate without simultaneously casting doubt on the logical-subject role of the term this predicate is attached to. For example, as Russell and Frege saw, if we are to say that 'exist'

D

in 'The devil does not exist' is not a logical predicate, then neither can 'the devil' here be a logical subject. It ought to have been noticed that similarly we cannot cast doubt on the predicative status of 'present', 'past', and 'future' without *ipso facto* casting doubt upon the right to regard as logical subjects (or proxies for logical subjects) the expressions that 'past', 'present', and 'future' are grammatically predicated of; but this realization has been pretty uncommon.

The point was however made clearly and emphatically in the works of Arthur Prior. He did see the difficulty about hanging on to the view that a phrase like 'the death of Queen Anne' can be a definite description, a logical subject or proxy for a logical subject, while rejecting the status of 'is present', 'is past', 'is future' as logical predicates. 'The death of Queen Anne' is called by modern grammarians a nominalization of a sentence. Of what sentence exactly? Clearly, one predicating some form of the verb 'to die' and having 'Queen Anne' as subject; but we need also a tense-determination. In a plainer way of speaking, and a way regarded by Prior as also logically more perspicuous, 'Queen Anne's death is past (future)' would be replaced by 'Queen Anne did (will) die'; and here the auxiliary verb 'did' or 'will' forms a verb out of a verb, a predicable expression out of a predicable expression. McTaggart went wrong in regarding tense-expressions as predicable in their own right and as standing for certain perceptible or imaginable characteristics. However, Prior's analysis leaves us with tensed verbs; and these are just as much expressions of *A*-characteristics as McTaggart took the terms 'past', 'present', and 'future' to be, for they are still tied to some specifiable present. We shall later see the importance of this.

What Prior can free us from, like a dream when a man awakes, is Mr Dunne's nightmarish vista of times beyond times *ad infinitum*. We need indeed a further piece of apparatus; besides tense-auxiliaries modifying verbs, we need the proposition-forming phrases 'It was the case that' and 'It will be the case that': the exact logical relations of these to tense-auxiliaries raise tricky logical problems, discussed by Prior, into which I cannot enter here. With these operators, we can simply represent e.g., 'The pastness of Geach's death is future' and 'The futurity of Queen Anne's death is past' by 'It will be the case that Geach did die' and, 'This was once the case: Queen Anne will die.' Such a monstrous idea as that there is a future slice of the history of an event, Geach's death, in which that event has the characteristic of pastness, melts away like a phantasm of the night; and with it vanishes Mr Dunne's idea of a second-order time in which first-order events themselves have things happening to them.

Mr Dunne, I fear, was ingeniously rationalizing the superstition that would have us take dreams as seriously as waking life or even more so. On this matter we dare not be tolerant towards a view involving relapse from civilization into barbarism. As Heraclitus said:

It is not meet to act and speak like men asleep.
The waking have one common world, but the sleeping turn aside each into a world of his own.
Those who speak with understanding must hold fast to what is common, as a city holds fast to its law, and even more strongly.

McTaggart had no truck with this or any other superstition fashionable among intellectuals. But his first argument to show that change involves the real occurrence of A-characteristics must be counted as a total failure, involving an error essentially similar to Mr Dunne's. If objects change from one state to another it simply does not follow that these states themselves would have to undergo a second-order change, from futurity through presentness to pastness.

McTaggart's second argument is much stronger: unless there are logically complete propositions of variable truth-value, there is no change; and the only such propositions that there are are ones involving A-characteristics. This is not weakened but strengthened if we take as expressing A-characteristics not just the terms 'past', 'present', and 'future', but also tensed verbs like 'will die' and 'did die' (317–18).

This argument has often been evaded by resort to propositions bringing in time-specifications such as philosophers schematically represent by 'at time t'. But such expressions nowise belong to our grass-roots temporal discourse. In C. S. Lewis's *Perelandra* the author describes an idyllic existence on the planet Venus; the bounty of Nature is such that the human-looking inhabitants need neither toil nor spin, nor need they keep appointments on the dot; the sky is perpetually covered with cloud, so that there are no heavenly bodies serving (as the Bible says) for signs and for seasons and for days and for years. But the rational animals on Venus need not therefore lack all temporal discourse; they would still be able to say 'now' and 'then', 'before' and 'after'. Basic temporal expressions would still be intelligible; but expressions of the type 'at time t' would be very difficult to translate into the language of Venus. To make sense of these, we men require an enormously complex set of empirical facts, which might well not have obtained and which indeed according to Einstein do not obtain quite as we used to think.

For example, so many rotations of the hour-hand of our clock correspond to so many rotations of the Earth, so much water running out of a water-clock, and so on. That these processes more or less keep time with one another, and with the revolutions of heavenly bodies round one another, is a complicated empirical matter; knowledge of this is not at all needed to understand grass-roots temporal discourse. It follows that analysis of temporal discourse at this primitive level is merely perverse if it brings in locutions of the 'at time t' sort, dependent as these are for their intelligibility upon facts nowise involved in primitive judgements of succession and simultaneity.

Now grass-roots temporal discourse just is framed in terms of past, present, and future tenses; and all temporal discourse appears to depend on this, logically and epistemologically. And on the face of it tensed propositions are propositions that vary in truth-value with time. So once again we should get the result that change is impossible unless A-characteristics really occur. Of course there are counter-arguments, as always happens in philosophy: I am trying only to show that here McTaggart has a good *prima facie* case.

Here I ought to mention a further point made by McTaggart: that without A-characteristics an object's having different qualities at different times could no more constitute change than its having different qualities in different spatial parts; in both cases there would be no change but only variegation (316). A poker, let us say, is now hot, now cold, now hot again. If we think of a mere order, in which a cold phase comes between two hot phases, how does this differ from the poker's being (say) hot at both ends but cold in the middle? No doubt we need to bring in a different dimension; but why should this be called a *time*-dimension? Only if we can say that the poker e.g. *was* hot and *will be* hot but *now is not* hot can we bring out what is distinctively temporal. Those who reject *A*-characteristics ought to say that time is a *delusion*: that we *misperceive* as temporal one of the dimensions in which the bodies and fields of the material universe are extended. And though nobody advocates such a view nakedly, many come close to it: Quine, for example, thinks that the difference between spatial and temporal extension is comparable to that between vertical and horizontal; both are observer-bound, neither has cosmic significance.

McTaggart, as we have seen already, dismisses this view that the so-called time-dimension is the way we misperceive one dimension in which material entities are extended. He did this in his discussion of Matter. He there argued that all material characteristics are as delusive as temporal ones; and the question whether his arguments against material characteristics have any validity does not at all turn on how many dimensions the material world is supposed to extend in.

McTaggart has also a third argument for *A*-characteristics' being indispensable for the reality of time. It is surprising how late this argument comes in *The Nature of Existence*, in fact only on p. 271 of vol. 2, in a footnote: surprising, because this argument if valid would render the other two superfluous. If *B*-characteristics actually need to be analysed in terms of *A*-characteristics, plainly *A*-characteristics will be unavoidable in an account of time. Now McTaggart argues that '*x* is earlier than *y*' *means*, 'Either *x* is past when *y* is present, or *x* is present when *y* is future' (610).

There are two objections to this analysis. First, 'when' appears to answer to a *B*-characteristic rather than an *A*-characteristic, so at least *B*-characteristics have not been reduced *without remainder* to *A*-characteristics. This would of course not show that *A*-characteristics are not indispensable in the analysis: and moreover Arthur Prior, pursuing McTaggart's line of thought, showed that 'when' itself can be analysed away in terms of expressions for *A*-characteristics and a plain non-temporal 'both ... and ...': '*x* is earlier than *y*' works out as, 'It either is or was or will be the case that both *x* is past and *y* is present.'

To this analysis it may then be further objected that it incorrectly uses 'present' and 'past' as logical predicates. But Prior would reply that, '*x* is past' and, '*y* is present' are just schematic representations of a past-tense and a present-tense clause. Let us take a concrete example: 'Hitler's death was earlier than Stalin's death.' We may spell this out as, 'The following either was, is, or will be the case: *both* Hitler has died *and* Stalin is dying.' And now there is no need of the bogus predicate-terms 'past' and 'present': but the *B*-relation of temporal succession has been analysed in terms of *A*-characteristics. It is arguable that such an analysis in terms of *A*-characteristics – ones expressed not by the pseudo-predicates 'past', 'present', and 'future' but by tensed verbs – is always possible, for all temporal discourse: and if so the indispensability of *A*-characteristics in an account of time will be manifest.

To sum up: I have given three arguments of McTaggart's to show that *B*-characteristics depend on *A*-characteristics. The first one, which has drawn a lot of artillery fire, is to my mind an extremely vulnerable argument. However, McTaggart can abandon this position without much loss. The other two arguments seem to me to be pretty strong ones. Suppose we agree with McTaggart thus far, that is, suppose that we agree that he showed 'No change, no time', and that change depends on the reality of *A*-characteristics. We now come to the nub of the question: are *A*-characteristics real, or are they merely delusory?

McTaggart has two arguments to show that *A*-characteristics are delusory. One is the less important of the two, but still of some importance to him; it arises from the odd question, 'How long is the present?' This is an old question; you find St Augustine torturing himself about it in his *Confessions*. If there is a succession, then surely only one little bit of the succession can be present; but then the succession gets in the end reduced to a knife-edge; you can follow this dialectic out in the *Confessions*. One answer to this, which seems to me frivolous, simply appeals to the fluctuating use of the present tense in ordinary language. It is pointed out that you can perfectly well say that Geach *is* lecturing in Philadelphia even at a time when I am not giving a lecture, and with reference to a span of time stretching over several weeks; or that Stokowski *is* conducting the Ninth Symphony, which again is something that necessarily takes a considerable time (nothing that he did in a knife-edge present could constitute conducting the Ninth Symphony); and so on. I think the elasticity of the ordinary-language present is not a sufficient answer to the puzzles that McTaggart raised about the specious present. For our specious present is, on the face of it, not something linguistic but something psychological.

Let us go back to Augustine. Augustine desperately tries to explain the difference between long and short time in terms of the number of things that I remember or anticipate. He considers a man reciting a poem that he knows by heart: more and more of the recitation of the poem is remembered recitation, less and less is anticipated recitation; this is how he explains long and short time. But now what are we to do about one of the things that Augustine himself mentions: the difference between the long and the short vowel? Is one to say that if I call a vowel long in pronunciation, it is a matter of a series of memories and a series of anticipations in regard to the pronunciation of *that vowel*, and this series is a longer series than if I were pronouncing a short vowel? This does not begin to look plausible. Surely we want to say that the difference between a long and short vowel is not something that is just a matter of memory and anticipation, as Augustine makes out; nor yet is it a matter of that elasticity in the use of the present tense to which the more recent philosophizing draws attention; it seems to be just given in experience that 'ā' is long and 'ă' is short.

How *can* this be given in experience? How can something that happens over a stretch of time be perceived *now*? Particularly if, as McTaggart argues, the very notion of earlier and later involved in temporal protraction has distinctions of past and present buried in it? It is difficult to believe that the specious present of our experience, with a duration that we seem to perceive, is anything *but* specious. For if there is a real non-momentary present, how long is this present? And if there is only a knife-edge present, does this conform at all to our experience of the present? This sort of difficulty makes McTaggart say that our experience of present happening, which is central to our ordinary notion of time, is for sure incurably subjective; and therefore, that the rejection of the reality of time is not so very paradoxical after all (344–5).

The other, more important, argument that McTaggart has is that the notion of *A*-characteristics' being real involves an outright contradiction. For example, on the one hand the truth of 'Queen Anne has died' involves that from *some* temporal point of view it is also true to say 'Queen Anne is dying', or 'Queen Anne will die'; and on the other hand, these different points of view, although in some way they necessarily imply one another, are likewise incompatible with one another. Now can we believe this is the way the world is: that it is in principle impossible to have one view of it that is simply true, but there are only a set of views, each justified on its own account but uncombinable with other equally justified views? McTaggart thought this was impossible, and rejected the reality of time if it should imply this (329).

This argument is followed in McTaggart's text (332) by a tricky attempted proof that a certain way in which we might try to remove the contradiction generates an infinite vicious regress. McTaggart's critics have said much about this: I shall say nothing. Wittgenstein once remarked that often when philosophers *think* the trouble is a vicious regress, the *real* trouble arises already at the first step: if it is rightly diagnosed there, we can forget about the regress. For example, in the Third Man argument, there is *already* a contradiction in affirming simultaneously (i) that there is *just one* Form in virtue of which each object covered by the general name 'man' is to be regarded as a man, and (ii) that since this Form also, indeed primarily, is called by the name 'man', there must be a *second* Form in virtue of which 'man' applies to the first Form and to each man commonly so called; there is absolutely no need for the further elaboration of the argument, in which Plato seeks to show that by parity of reasoning we get an infinite series of Forms. So here: if McTaggart's alleged contradiction is bogus, we need not consider whether the attempt to remove it would generate a vicious regress; if it is not bogus, it suffices to show that *A*-characteristics are not objective.

To get over the full force of McTaggart's paradox, I recommend an article by Michael Dummett, 'A defence of McTaggart's proof of the unreality of time', which shows also the superficiality and inadequacy of those attacks on McTaggart which appeal to the parallelism between 'now' and 'here' (*Philosophical Review*, vol. 69, p. 497). It is perfectly easy to conceive of an observer who contemplates the whole of a space without himself being located in that space; as Wittgenstein said in the *Tractatus*, the eye isn't anywhere *in* the visual field. We can thus imagine, so to say, an eye of God which looks upon *all* space impartially. Can we also imagine an eye of God which looks upon all time impartially?

People have often talked like that. Aquinas talks about God looking upon the series of travellers in time from the stronghold of eternity (*ex arce aeternitatis*): what on the level of the travellers looks like a succession, from the high citadel of eternity looks like a series spread out and simultaneously viewable. I don't think this will do at all. It is impossible, Dummett forcibly argued in the article I've just cited, to get a view of the Universe which is complete and which does not specify *when* it is, what bit of the Universe is *now*. To the protest that there is no privileged set of observers, I reply in a rather flat and dull way, but I think truly, that of course there are privileged observers, namely the ones who are living and observing right now. And to the protest that physics doesn't mention any *now*, I have an even duller, and indeed an old-fashioned Scholastic, answer. Physics or any science abstracts from the *now*, because it is out to make statements of general law; but that doesn't mean that there isn't any *now* to be abstracted from.

It is interesting that on this matter of the reality of the present, Aquinas's view seems to have oscillated somewhat; for side by side with this talk, to my mind radically unsatisfactory, about the citadel of eternity, Aquinas also says things, even about God, that clearly require the reality of A-characteristics. For example, statements about God's power essentially need to be temporally qualified; for if Miss X has already lost her virginity, there's nothing that even Almighty God can do about that. (The example is Aquinas's own.) Before she fell, God could have prevented it; now that it has happened, preventing it no longer falls under the concept (*ratio*) of things that can be done, and on that account is not anything that even God can do. It would involve a contradiction that God should undo what has once been done (*Summa Theologica*, I, q.25 art. 4). Here Aquinas strongly asserts the reality of what McTaggart would call A-characteristics, in contrast to his own seeming attempt to play them down with talk about the citadel of eternity. I cannot here explore further this area in the history of medieval philosophy.

Getting back to McTaggart, I think the strength of his argument is, as Dummett has argued, an idea, a strong prejudice we have, that there must be possible some sort of complete neutral view of this Universe. If there logically could be such a view, as not only believers in the Divine contemplation of the Universe as a whole have held, then A-characteristics cannot really occur; and if A-characteristics cannot really occur, then, I must agree with McTaggart, there cannot be any real time or change either. What McTaggart says there *is*, is a real series of things which is misperceived as a series of successive events; the series itself is real enough, and when one event seems to come in-between two other events, the realities that are being misperceived really do come in just that order. What the order is, and what its ordering relation is, in reality, will be subjects for our future discussion, if McTaggart will allow us the phrase.

I conclude by showing that on McTaggart's own footing we do not so easily escape the threat of contradiction by denying the reality of time. For as we saw in Chapter 2, by way of drawing limits to scepticism McTaggart several times uses this style of argument: If there even delusively appears to be X, there really is X: so we cannot consistently hold that there *only* appears to be X. He argues this way taking 'X' to be 'error', 'pain', and 'pleasure' (510, 857, 858): we cannot without contradiction say that we *only appear* to fall into error, endure pain, or enjoy pleasure, and do not really do so. Now however delusive our experiences may be, we have delusions when coexistence is impossible: I cannot, e.g. *at once* have a pleasant delusion marred by anticipation of what I regard as immediately future pain, *and* a painful delusion aggravated by thoughts of what I regard as past joy. If I even *have* these delusions, they must *be*, as they appear to be, successive. So even if McTaggart's arguments against the reality of time appeared conclusive, even then, since by his own pattern of reasoning we can construct what appear to be equally conclusive arguments that the unreality of time leads to contradiction too, we had better stay with the common-sense view.

8 Persons and mental states

McTaggart defines spirit, or spiritual substance, as substance whose content is entirely the content of one or more persons (381). We can understand what this means only when we have examined McTaggart's account of persons and his view of what the content of a person is.

McTaggart uses 'personality' as an abstract noun, but 'self' as the corresponding concrete noun. This is, to my mind, a stylistic blemish; moreover, some philosophers have used the word 'self' in very dubious ways, and this may create a prejudice against McTaggart. In fact his meaning is nowise altered if we replace 'self' by 'person' throughout, and I shall henceforth keep to the word 'person'. This has the added advantage that we can stipulate once for all that in such compounds as 'self-consciousness' the first element is not the noun meaning 'person' but a reflexive pronoun; I do not think McTaggart was misled by the possible ambiguity of 'self-' in such compounds.

As is well known, various philosophers, notably Hume and William James, have maintained that there is no such thing as self-perception: upon looking within there is found nothing identifiable as the very person who is taking a look. McTaggart sought to show they were mistaken. He did not do this by a claim to have managed the feat of self-perception through better observational technique; rather, his argument is transcendental in the Kantian sense; it arises from the question, 'How are judgements about oneself possible – judgements naturally expressed in the first person singular?' Such judgements, he holds, are possible only if each of us perceives himself as a person having certain characteristics (393). His argument is confessedly an expanded version of one sketched in Russell's famous essay, 'Knowledge by acquaintance and knowledge by description'. In

Russell's terminology, each of us has to be acquainted with himself as a person, and does not merely think of himself under some definite description.

Russell at this time held, and McTaggart borrowed from him, the view that the objects of acquaintance include abstract characteristics, and that introspection reveals to us acts of simple awareness of characteristics – e.g. a bare awareness of equality apart from any thought of one thing's being equal to another. This is a mirky doctrine, inherited, I suspect, from the equally mirky Scholastic doctrine of 'simple apprehension' as one of the acts of the intellect. And no awarenesses of characteristics need be assumed to exist except as inseparable parts of thoughts relating to those characteristics. McTaggart thus diminishes the force of his argument about 'I' by an ill-chosen example: the judgement a man may express by, 'I am aware of equality.' One may well doubt whether any genuine judgement is thus expressed. We can however forget about the example: a careful reading shows that McTaggart's argument does not depend on it. It is quite easy to re-formulate the argument so as to show that if valid it will work regarding *any* judgement concerning oneself, expressible in the first person singular; we need not confine ourselves to introspective judgements, nor to psychological judgements, nor to judgements that are either true or well-founded. If valid at all, McTaggart's argument will show that no first-person judgement is even *possible* unless there is self-perception.

Suppose, for example, that Smith judges, or even considers the supposition, 'I am fat.' Smith is then *ipso facto* in a position to know directly that one and the same person both is ascribing fatness to somebody and is having fatness ascribed to him; if he were not in a position to know this, he could not understand 'I am fat' as opposed to 'Someone is fat.' But the characteristics of ascribing fatness and of being a person to whom fatness is ascribed are logically independent; that they *ever* go together can only be an empirical matter. How then is Smith in a position to know directly that they go together? Plainly Smith needs no further *evidence* to establish this. McTaggart's reply is that Smith knows what is meant by 'I' because he can perceive himself, and thus in particular can perceive himself as being both a person to whom fatness is being ascribed and a person ascribing fatness, because he can perceive himself as judging about himself.

McTaggart emphasizes that the sense of 'I' cannot be given by any definite description that in fact applies to the speaker. On this point I believe he was right. To bring out the point further, let us consider the situation at the beginning of the play *Oedipus Rex*. Oedipus is in fact the slayer of Laios, and he is in a state of mind describable thus:

1   Oedipus judges that the slayer of Laios is hateful to the Gods. We may accordingly say of Oedipus either of the following:
2   Oedipus judges concerning the slayer of Laios that he is hateful to the Gods,
3   Oedipus judges concerning Oedipus that he is hateful to the Gods – Oedipus' judgement strikes Oedipus though he doesn't know it.

And from 3 we may further infer:

4   Oedipus judges concerning himself that he is hateful to the Gods. Here 'himself' is the ordinary, or as grammarians say the *direct*, reflexive pronoun: 3 and 4 are related just like 'Oedipus blinded Oedipus' and 'Oedipus blinded himself'.

But we cannot infer:

5   Oedipus judges that he himself is hateful to the Gods. Here 'himself' is the *indirect* reflexive – the proxy in indirect speech for the 'I' in the direct speech, 'I am hateful to the Gods.' Oedipus is not making *this* judgement. 4, or equivalently 3, would be true if Oedipus thought of himself in *any* particular way and judged that the person *so* thought of was hateful to the Gods; thus 3 and 4 do follow from 5, but not conversely; even if 5 is false, 4 may none the less be true, as following from 1 and the premise 'Oedipus is the slayer of Laios'. The kind of judgement reported in 5 likewise cannot be reduced to the kind reported in 1; for whatever definite description 'the *D*' may be, 'Oedipus judges that the *D* is hateful to the Gods' will not yield 5 unless we have an extra premise,

'Oedipus knows or believes that he himself is the *D*' – and this brings us back to the 'he himself' construction that we were seeing if we could analyse away.

Let us now consider the predicable '——— believes that he will get the Chair of Latin.' This is of course ambiguous in a way that would have to be contextually resolved: we need to know which Chair vacancy is in question. But given this information, the ambiguity is resolved; the sense of what we are predicating does not depend on which subject of predication is supplied, and so we have here something that may be true univocally of a number of people. Contrast this with the example, borrowed from Quine: '——— was so called because of his size.' If we can truly say, concerning a certain artist and a certain companion of Robin Hood, 'Giorgione was so called because of his size and Little John was so called because of his size,' we are not predicating the same thing of the two men; the adverb 'so' replaces quotation of 'Giorgione' in one case and of 'Little John' in the other; Giorgione was called 'Giorgione', and Little John was called 'Little John', because of his size. It would be nonsense to say: 'More than one man was so called because of his size.' But it is perfectly sensible to say 'More than one man believes he (himself) will get the Chair of Latin'; if this is truly said, two men will have, in a sense, *the same* belief (even though both cannot be believing rightly!).

To use Frege's terminology, what *A* or *B* believes when he thinks he himself will get the Chair of Latin is determined by the sense of the sentence, 'I shall get the Chair of Latin' when said by *A* or *B* as the case may be. Now the sense of a sentence depends not only on who is referred to, *A* or *B*, but also on the way *A* or *B* is presented to the mind – the *Art des Gegebenseins*. However, Frege himself says in his essay, 'The thought' ('Der Gedanke'), that each of us is presented to *his own* thought in a peculiar and incommunicable way. In general, reference does not determine sense, the manner of presentation; but let us suppose – as Frege seems to – that the reference of 'I' *does* determine its sense. Then the sense of, 'I shall get the Chair of Latin' will be fixed given *who* the speaker is; it will be a definite function of the reference of 'I'. And accordingly what each person who believes he himself will get the Chair of Latin does believe will not be the same thing for each person; but there will be a definite function, with the holder of the belief as argument, whose value is that which each of these hopeful candidates believes; *that* is what all who so believe have in common.

Frege's doctrines are not wholly satisfactory; but I think some modified form of them is needed to clear up the puzzle of how and in what sense each of several people can have *the same* belief about himself as another of them has. And this brings us by another road to McTaggart's central contention: what self-knowledge is for a man is determined simply by *who* he is, and is not knowledge of him as satisfying some description. We see also how *A* can understand what *B* means by 'I', even if *A* knows *B* only by description: the thought that *B* expresses by 'I am so-and-so' will be a certain function of *B*, and the thought *A* expresses in those words is the same function of *A*, and *A* can know this.

Here, as Wittgenstein might have said, very quickly the conjuring trick is performed. The use of 'I' is not to be assimilated or reduced to the use of any proper name or definite description, that is true, but to call a person's knowledge of himself 'perception' suggests – and is meant by McTaggart to suggest – that it may be assimilated to his perception of external objects. In this transition of thought, McTaggart was of course not deliberately playing a trick; he was merely unaware of what a big and crucial step he was taking right here. But this is the point which one might say is very dubious.

Many philosophers who have written about self-knowledge have assumed that nobody can directly perceive anybody other than himself as a person (even if he can perceive himself as a person, which not everybody has admitted); and if they have used this misleading model of perception, the inner eye, they have pretty generally held that this eye can gaze only upon the contents of one's own mind (the beetle in the box). By a sure instinct, the Absolute's family solicitor, whose advice was always listened to with respect and followed with advantage as regards the investments of his own College, did not invest any of his own intellectual capital in this unsound stock. We find extremely little in McTaggart on the subject of privacy; in the chapter on Spirit, or equivalently the article on 'Personality' in the *Encyclopaedia of Religion and Ethics*, McTaggart just says that he doesn't see *any* reason why a person should not perceive other persons and the state of other persons. Indeed, it is positively a *requirement* of his philosophy that in absolute reality, however things may presently appear to be, each person *does* perceive, directly perceive, other persons and the states of mind of other persons.

Let us for a moment imagine McTaggart encountering some young spark who had imbibed a dose of *Wittgensteinerei*, and who tells him that we *do* observe other people's anger, surprise, disappointed expectation, etc. McTaggart would say: 'Well, why not? My philosophy positively *requires* that this should be so. It is true that when I wrote my book, I thought that though this was true in absolute reality, it was contrary to our *prima facie* impression of the world; I thought our *prima facie* impression of the world would be that we only made *judgements* about other people, and did not *perceive* them and their states. Still, if you could show the contrary, your conclusion is welcome to me; it diminishes the division between the way my theory requires that things have to be in absolute reality and the way things appear to be in present experience.' In this necessarily brief presentation of McTaggart's views, we can leave it at that. We can see why the question of privacy, which has bulked so large in philosophical psychology for so many years, played a wholly negligible part in McTaggart's thought.

Our next concern is the content of a person. Many people who have held that we could establish metaphysically the existence of persons, have held that a person either is, or has as his ontic core, something called a pure ego; this has no internal structure, and undergoes no succession of states in time, and so on; it is a sort of spiritual atom. The temptation to believe in a pure ego is very much like the temptation to believe in other philosophical chimeras which I discussed earlier on: the temptation to believe in a bare particular, which, as you might say, doesn't have any qualities because *it* is what *has* them, or in prime matter, which never *has* any form at any time precisely because *it* is what *underlies* the change of form, etc., etc. McTaggart rejected bare particulars, so of course he rejected the idea of a pure ego; in fact in the passage of *The Nature of Existence* I am presently discussing, he doesn't even mention the pure ego, he passes over this theory with silent contempt (and quite right too).

McTaggart held the very opposite view: the content of a person consists wholly of that person's mental states; and speaking in terms of time, that would be his successive states as well as his simultaneous states. There is nothing *to* a person, except his successive and simultaneous states; he has internal structure and content in respect of his states, his states are not just relationships he temporarily enters into. Let us consider McTaggart's example of a detective who knows that someone is a murderer, or a man who knows that the potato on his plate is rotten; causally, of course, this is more likely to influence the fate of the murderer or the potato than of the detective or the disgruntled diner; but if you consider just the fact that so-and-so is being thought about, this is a fact that makes a real difference to the detective or the disgruntled diner, and doesn't of itself make a difference to the murderer or the potato. If thinking-about were a relation, this would be inexplicable; but if there is an actual element in the make-up of a person which *is* the detective's thought about the murderer, or the diner's thought about the potato, then this asymmetry is readily explained (412).

If we compare McTaggart's theory of the person with Hume's 'bundle' theory, what does the difference amount to? McTaggart might have said that Hume simply didn't see the wood for the trees. But this is too easy. Even for Hume it is not just that there are various mental states, what Hume called 'perceptions' and 'ideas', existing as separate and (*sub specie temporis*) short-lived individuals; these states are parts of a whole, with properties of its own, just as from an aeroplane you can see the shape of the forest, which is not the shape of any tree by itself. Further, the mental states entering into the make-up of a person change, just as the population of trees constituting a forest changes from generation to generation.

The difference between McTaggart and Hume is that McTaggart

thinks a person is ontologically prior to the states which are differentiations of his unity (indeed a state has to be identified via the person whose state it is, and cannot be identified in any other way); it is, for McTaggart, a manifestly incoherent thought to try to think of floating ideas, or states of mind that are not anybody's state of mind in particular. Again, if there are two forests close to one another it might be a matter of decision whether you said that an outlying tree belonged to the one forest or to the other, or was just a straggler on its own; but there could be no such situation about states of mind; a state of mind has to be the state of mind of a definite person, and then cannot be also somebody else's state of mind.

A fortiori, then, one person cannot be a part of another person, because in that case, all states of mind of the one person would be states of mind also of the other person. So McTaggart rejects the idea, which some idealists went in for, that there is a super-person, a God or Absolute, of whom finite persons are parts, whether temporary or permanent.

That then, is what people are made of; people are made of their own mental states. And mental states, as we saw, are for McTaggart the *entire* content of any given person. In his general account of mental states, he starts out from a curious tripartite division of mental life into the cogitative, the appetitive, and the emotional: thinking, willing, feeling – there are various terminologies for this alleged tripartite division. I have never clearly understood the rationale of this division, and I do not know how far it goes back; you certainly get it in Kant, but I do not know its prehistory, it is certainly not found in Plato or Aristotle or the medievals. As we shall see, McTaggart thinks that he can show without appealing to his own special philo-sophy that this classification is not quite right, but he thinks it is *prima facie* right.

By volition, McTaggart wants to cover everything that would be called '*volitio*' in medieval times; and thus not only what are called 'volitions' or 'acts of will' in modern philosophy – the mental acts that directly initiate changes in the world. About these, understandably, he has very little to say; the character-istic of being a volition in this sense must be a delusive characteristic; there are no mental acts with the characteristic of initiating changes in the world, because there are no changes in the world. McTaggart's 'volition' corresponds to the appetitive, or as it is sometimes called the conative, aspect of mental life. 'Emotion', I imagine, is fairly self-explanatory.

For the apprehensive side of the mind McTaggart uses distinctively the terms 'cognition' and 'cogitation'. The latter is the *summum genus*, subdivided as shown below.

Classification of cogitations

	cognitive		*non-cognitive*
Intuitive (non-propositional)	awareness	{ of characteristics { of individuals (=perception)	imaging
Discursive (propositional)	judgement		assumption

If we ignore awarenesses of characteristics for the moment, we get a neat quadripartite row-and-column classification of what he called 'cogitations'. He uses 'cognition' distinctively for those cogitations that can be correct or erroneous; for he does not think all can be. He holds that a mere thought (let us say) that pigs have wings, is neither correct nor erroneous. Only a thought that is assented to, or in other words a judgement, is correct or erroneous. Similarly, whereas perceptions can be correct or erroneous, imaging differs from perception precisely in this respect: an imaging is neither correct nor erroneous – if there is a thing just like what I image, then the imaging is not on that account correct; if there is no such thing, the imaging is not on that account erroneous. He speaks of the mental state as an 'imaging', and of the thing imaged as an 'imaginatum' – he avoids, in technical contexts, both the noun 'imagination' and the verb 'to imagine'. He rightly says that 'to imagine' often means 'to make a supposition which is contrary to facts' and then has nothing at all to do with the forming of mental images.

We may notice that there is no place in this classification for anything like acts of understanding or acts of knowing. The problem of knowledge and belief which has caused so much agitation in the Oxford contemporaries of McTaggart never seems to have worried him at all. He just says blandly, without any sort of argument, that 'to know' is 'to believe truly'. He does not seem, indeed, to have worried about problems of epistemology, scepticism, etc., at all. He had an epigram to the effect that all we can say in general about man's powers of knowing things is that men are capable of error and also capable of correcting it. You get into absurdity if you say that perhaps all human beliefs are false; and you also get into absurdity if you say that perhaps all human beliefs are true, as Protagoras may have said. And so we live in a mixed state of knowledge and error, and we have ways of correcting false steps. The general problem of scepticism, and again problems of whether there is such a thing as *absolutely* certain knowledge, and whether acts of knowledge are distinguished from acts of believing by some introspective criterion – all of this seems to have bothered McTaggart extremely little.

Perhaps owing to my introduction to McTaggart's works at an early and impressionable age, I have a strong sympathy with him; I should wish to undermine the Oxford position, as I may call it, about knowledge and belief. Suppose that some of our cognitions are knowledge, and others are mere judgement or belief, *and* that there is some introspective criterion by which we can tell which is which. According to the Oxford position, whenever I know, I am certain; but sometimes when I am certain, I don't know, I am merely taking things for granted. All the same, if I am certain, I cannot simultaneously doubt; and so long as my certainty continues, I shall not apply the introspective criterion to tell whether I have got a genuine certainty, which is knowledge, or a bogus certainty, which is a taking-for-granted; so just when I need the criterion, it is of no use to me; it is not, therefore, *any* use to me.

Moreover, with later sophistication, I should argue that the very idea of an act of knowledge is a muddle, because the verb 'to know' is logically akin to the verb 'to be able': the claim to know is the claim to have a certain ability (and so, for that matter, is the claim to understand), and therefore to postulate acts of knowing (and acts of understanding) is simply to have mislocated the logical category of psychological verbs. In any event, as I said, McTaggart had no place in the system for either acts of knowing or acts of understanding.

That he had a place for episodic judgements, as opposed to dispositional beliefs, might again strike some people as an extremely dubious feature in his system; but I should defend him about this. Whenever a man answers a question, or is faced with a problem and comes up with a solution, that is, whenever he answers a question for which he has to *think* of the answer (not e.g. when a sober man is asked for his name and address), then he is performing an act of judging. I think, therefore, that there continually *are* acts of judging, and not only dispositions of belief.

The difference between judgements and assumptions, as McTaggart calls them, is not a difference in their content or internal structure, but a difference in their assertoric force. Both judgements and assumptions are discursive or propositional; which judgement or assumption a man has would be described by using a 'that'-clause: '*A* is judging that so-and-so', '*A* is assuming that so-and-so.' To this extent, judgements and assumptions are just alike, but they differ in the indefinable respect that a judgement is assertoric and an assumption is not; this means that you stick your neck out if you make a judgement, and can be accused of error, but not if you just make an assumption.

All of this is just *prima facie*, let me emphasize; McTaggart is classifying the kinds of mental states that *appear* in introspection to exist. Introspection for him is itself a case of perception; and perception can be, and often is, misperception. McTaggart thinks that we have sense-perceptions of the external world, and also introspective perceptions of ourselves and our own mental states; he is making a big assumption in taking it that the same term 'perception' applies in both cases. This assumption has been conspicuously challenged since Wittgenstein; but I am not going to go into this – it would take us too far from McTaggart.

The kinds of thing that you can perceive, you can also image. I can image, form a mental picture of, the door behind my head, though I cannot now see it, and again of things that I did see in the past, though I don't see them now; and McTaggart thinks there can also be introspective images of mental states, just as there are introspective perceptions of mental states. I can, e.g. 'image' Cromwell's contempt for the Young Pretender, although there was not any such thing as Cromwell's contempt for the Young Pretender (and although if there had been such a mental state it would anyhow have been Cromwell's mental state and not mine). But just as I can perceive my own contempt for somebody when I am in a state of contempt, and can remember my own contempt, so I can 'image' somebody else's contempt.

Memory, by the way, McTaggart holds to consist in simultaneously imaging something and judging that that is how things were; thus memory is not a separate class of mental state, but can be reduced to imaging and judging.

There is a striking difference between the internal structure that judgements and assumptions, on the one hand, appear to have, and the internal structure that perceptions and images, on the other hand, appear to have. A judgement has a structure, or appears introspectively to have a structure, which corresponds in some ways to the structure of a sentence in which the judgement would naturally be expressed. How far this can be pressed might be doubted. In the theory of judgement that I myself sketched in *Mental Acts*, I argued that whereas we might recognize as constituents of a judgement individual Ideas, corresponding to words or phrases of sentences in which the judgement was expressed, on the contrary the main operator of a sentence, that is, the one or many-place predicate of a predicative sentence or some other such main operator bonding the sentence together, would *not* have corresponding to it any element in a judgement, but rather a relation relating together the Ideas which are constituents of the judgement. By this notion, I was trying to overcome certain difficulties that arise over Russell's 'multiple relation' theory of judgement. But however that may be, a judgement will certainly be naturally regarded as having an internal structure which to some extent corresponds to the words in which the judgement would be sententially expressed. The same goes for assumptions.

Characteristics enter into perceptions in quite another way. Perception of an individual substance is obviously perception of a substance *as* having qualities, and *as* having relations to other substances. And this does not mean merely perception of a substance *that has* qualities, or *that has* relations to other substances; it is perception of a substance *as* having qualitative and relational characteristics. It is fairly clear that you need not perceive all of the characteristics that an individual thing you perceive in fact has. In trying to set up a notion of prehension, the sense-datum philosophers seem to have had some inclination to make out that to prehend an object as being ABC is just to prehend an object that is in fact ABC. 'Prehension' comes from the Latin word for 'grasp'; now if I grasp a round smooth coin in my hand, that is enough to say, and the question whether I grasp it *as* round or *as* smooth or *as* of Tiberius Caesar wouldn't arise; if I grasp it, then I grasp a coin *that is* round and smooth and of Tiberius Caesar. But this notion of 'prehension' that sense-datum philosophers tried to set up is, I think, incoherent. To be sure, by cutting down the characteristics that a sense-datum has, they tried to make it possible for a person to grasp *all* the characteristics that it in fact has; they wished to make out that prehension not only is free from error but also comprehends *all* the characteristics of the data. I think this attempted construction was an incoherent one. Anyhow McTaggart had no such idea about perception. If we can see a thing as ABC, that does not mean that all that it is is ABC, and it does not mean that it even has to be ABC at all: we may be misperceiving.

To sum up: we perceive a thing, not just naked, but *as* having characteristics; to affirm that a thing is so perceived neither is entailed by nor entails the proposition that the thing in question actually has those characteristics. McTaggart further thinks that there are given in perception certain characteristics *of* characteristics. When one is perceiving A as red and B as green, it can be given in perception that these two colours are incompatible. This is the sort of grasp of things which his Cambridge contemporary W. E. Johnson called 'intuitive induction'. You can see in a particular case, say in a geometrical figure, that something that holds in this figure is in fact a general implication – what McTaggart called an 'intrinsic determination'. This alleged feature of perception, that the implication or intrinsic determination of characteristics can be grasped in it, is something that McTaggart makes much use of in further developing his theory (301).

Whereas a judgement ostensibly has a structure corresponding to the structure of the words in which it is expressed more or less, a perception has a radically different structure; the complexity of a perception, the way it *has* structure or parts, corresponds precisely to the way it *represents the object perceived* as having parts. A perception or imaging of something complex is a complex imaging and perception, just in that way and to that extent. Here there is a great kinship between what McTaggart says and some of the things Hume says; remember the passage in Hume's *Treatise* concerning the inner world of sun, moon and stars and the outer world (Everyman edition, p. 230f.). Hume is using this alleged parallelism in order to deny the simplicity of the self or soul, which was used as a basis for inferring its immortality and immateriality: McTaggart of course does not want the soul or person to be simple. Not only is a person complex, as consisting of mental states, but the person's perceptions themselves are complex, just in the way that they represent the object perceived as complex. If I perceive an object as consisting of parts, then my perception has parts corresponding to the way it represents the object as differentiated. The same goes for imaging – imagings have an internal structure corresponding to that of perceptions; but in McTaggart's sense of the word, they are not cognitive, i.e. they are not either knowledge or error.

Judgements and assumptions resemble each other and differ from perceptions in two main ways. First, a judgement about a whole W does not in general contain judgements about parts of W, whereas a perception of a whole as having parts has perceptions of the parts as parts of itself. Secondly, on the face of it a judgement can be indefinite in a way that a perception cannot; you can judge that an object of perception has some characteristic without judging that it has a determinate form of that characteristic, but in perception (according to a very common view, which McTaggart shares e.g. with Berkeley, Hume and Russell), characteristics are given in a determinate form. To use McTaggart's own illustration: I can see a man's iris only if I see it as having some definite colour: but I can judge that it was coloured without thinking of any specific colour. What goes for judgements here goes also for assumptions.

Imaging is on the face of it like perception and unlike judgement and assumption in these respects. Just as perception of a complex whole has as parts perceptions of the parts, so an imaging of a complex whole has as parts imagings of the parts; and again when imaging a thing as having a characteristic we must image it as having some perfectly determinate form of the characteristic. (Berkeley and Hume would certainly have maintained this along with McTaggart.) We shall see that difficulties arise for McTaggart about there being real judgements and assumptions, because (he argues) they cannot satisfy the requirement that every real individual has parts within parts *ad infinitum*, whereas perceptions can. No such difficulty arises for imagings; so far as this goes, there could be real imagings and not just introspective misperceptions of oneself as imagining.

McTaggart however argues that when there appears to be an imaging, there is no real imaging in the mind, but only a perception or several perceptions, introspectively misperceived as an imaging. He points out that we do not just image some set of characteristics as going together, any more than we just perceive a coincidence of characteristics; we perceive or image an *individual* (a 'substance') *as* having the characteristics. But in the case of imaging, how do we get at the individual that is imaged as having the various characteristics – say, as being red, oblong, and glossy? Imaging is a non-discursive experience; so the individual object of imaging must be given to the imaging person in perception, not by description. Yet we do not *seem* to be perceiving in the act of imaging; so here already there must be an introspective error. McTaggart concludes that there is only an introspective appearance of there being an act of imaging at all; the objects of apparent imagings are really objects of perceptions, and these perceptions are introspectively misrepresented as imagings.

It seems to me that McTaggart here goes wrong over the logic of intentional verbs. If I image a 3p stamp, he is saying, I image some individual (as being a) 3p stamp. But similarly if I want a 3p stamp, I want – and I shall be satisfied only if I get – some

individual 3p stamp. It does not follow that there is some individual 3p stamp that I want, even if I am in the post office with
a sheet of 3p stamps before my eyes; nor need there be some
individual that I want 'as' (want to be?) a 3p stamp. The question 'Which individual stamp do you want?' need have no
answer; neither need there be an answer to 'Which one do you
image?' Philosophy does make advances; the logic of intentionality is still by no means clear, but we now see pitfalls to which
McTaggart was blind, as all his generation in England were.

McTaggart's theories of desire and emotion may fairly be
taken together. His main thesis was one tentatively put forward
by Moore in a MIND review: namely, that a desire or emotion
with a given object is not a separate mental occurrence based
upon a previous or simultaneous apprehension ('cogitation') of
the object; rather, we must hold that our thoughts, perceptions,
etc. come so to say either penny plain or twopence coloured.
The 'colour' of thoughts, their volitional or emotional quality,
might be graphically represented as follows. Imagine a great
book in which a man's successive thoughts are written down in
the form of sentences: the content of the thought (what it is a
thought about) would be represented by the words that were
printed; the emotional or desiring attitude with which the
thought came would be represented by the colour of ink in which
the words were printed, and plain black ink would be used if the
thought had no emotional colouring. This, I think, gives a very
simple model for McTaggart's view of emotion and volition.
Desire of tea is to think 'Soon, I shall be having tea' desiringly.
And if I hope for my tea, that is to think 'Soon, I shall be having tea' hopefully. 'Soon I shall be seeing that man again,'
thought fearfully, is fear of seeing that man again. And so on.

This is an attractive theory, which seems neat and tidy;
however, it runs into difficulties. The difficulty arises chiefly out
of a point McTaggart himself made with regard to emotions,
introducing a very fundamental and important concept. An
emotion towards an object may be *in respect of* a characteristic.
This is quite different from its being *because of* a characteristic:
an emotion's being in respect of a characteristic is not a causal
fact. If I admire a man in respect of being courageous, what

causes my admiration? Is it my belief that he was courageous? But I don't admire him for being believed by me to be courageous; so it is not the characteristic of *being believed by me to be* courageous that is the characteristic in respect of which I admire him; it is the characteristic of *being* courageous that is the characteristic in respect of which I admire him. Moreover, this characteristic is one which, after all, he need not have; I may admire him in respect of his being courageous, when he really isn't courageous, but I only think he is.

This seems to be a very important notion to have got out explicitly. In a paper I once wrote on the *Euthyphro*,[1] I gave this notion a particular application: namely, there seems to be a general principle that a certain sort of reflexiveness about this 'in respect of' is impossible. You cannot, for example, admire a man *in respect of* his being admired by yourself (just that). 'What do I admire him for? Just *for* being admired by *me*!' This sort of reflexiveness with 'in respect of' appears, from case to case, to be absurd; and this is the point of one of the arguments in the *Euthyphro*. It cannot be that the Gods love pious conduct *for* being loved by the Gods, *in respect of* being loved by the Gods; but they love it in respect of its being pious; so the characteristic of piety must be different from the characteristic of being loved by the Gods. (Plato does not indeed at all explicitly distinguish this 'in respect of' sense of the preposition 'for' from the causal 'for'.)

If a thing is 'cognized' or 'cogitated' as having characteristics XYZ, it may be, say, admired in respect of being X and Y, and disliked in respect of being Z. But if you think of the emotional quality as something like a colour of a thought, how can this colour, colour the thought *qua* thought of the thing's being XY and not *qua* thought of its being Z? If the thought has constituents or internal structure corresponding to the structure of the sentence expressing it, perhaps this makes sense. You could, after all, write down the sentence 'He is XYZ,' and write 'X' and 'Y' in letters of gold, and 'Z' in some sort of dirty brown, to show which characteristics were the ones for which he was

[1] This is now reprinted as essay 1.4 in my book *Logic Matters* (Blackwell, 1972).

admired, and which were disapproved of. But according to McTaggart, if you perceive a thing as being *XYZ*, you would not have this perception splitting up into a perception of the thing as *XY* and a simultaneous perception of the same thing as being *Z*; there is only *one* perception, and if it is divided into parts, they correspond to the *parts* of the object, and not to the different *characteristics* of the object. So a perception does not have parts corresponding to the different characteristics of the thing; and yet there may be different emotional and desiderative attitudes towards a *perceived* object, according to the different *perceived* characteristics.

To use a bit of jargon, what McTaggart has been trying to do is to reduce the intentionality of desire and emotion to the intentionality of judgement and perception. It was a brave try, but I am not at all sure that it comes off, because this 'in respect of' business at least appears to let in an intentionality of desire and emotion distinct from and irreducible to the intentionality of thinking and perceiving. And with that I shall have to leave this very tricky problem. That there should be a satisfactory answer from McTaggart's point of view is not to be expected, in view of the very little way that discussions of intentionality had advanced in the philosophical world of McTaggart's time.

There is another important question about desire, which McTaggart raises and to which he gives a definite answer. He raises two questions; (a) Are there two sorts of judgements: affirming and denying? (b) Are there two sorts of appetition: desire and aversion? The two would be polar opposites in each case. He answers both questions in the negative. He says that what is judged, or what is desired, may be a negative assumed fact (or contemplated set-up), but that the judging and desiring is always the same.

I should like to say that there is *not* a polar opposition of affirmation and denial in the realm of judging, but that there *is* a distinction of polarly opposite attitudes in the realm of desire: desire and aversion are different attitudes, not just attitudes with describably different objects. The arguments by which people have tried to set up affirming and denying as polarly opposite attitudes in regard to thinking or judging seem to me to be unsatisfactory or confused and completely impede proper logical understanding of negation. As I have said,[1] there was a time when Christians and Muslims used to call one another 'unbelievers'. Now the situation of Christians and Muslims was not that one side went in for the activity of believing and the other for the activity of unbelieving; nor was it a question which side went in for which, that being what they disagreed about. The natural and clearly right way to describe the situation was that they believed different things, and incompatible things; if what the Christians believed was true, then what the Muslims believed was false, and vice versa. But it was not that one side was performing acts of believing and the other side performing acts of unbelieving.

This is rather important, because people maintain, especially with regard to religious belief, that belief is something like a favouring attitude towards what is believed. This, like lots of bad thinking, depends, as Wittgenstein would say, on an unbalanced diet of examples; people must be taking their examples from rather bland religions, in which what as part of his religion the believer takes to exist are good things; they forget that people have believed that the world is governed by fearful deities who want children passed through the fire, or that it is the battlefield of co-equal and co-eternal good and evil deities. Even if men believe that there is a good supreme God, they may also believe in other supernatural beings who are bad and hate mankind; and to these the believer may not have a favouring attitude at all.

It is a radically wrong idea about believing, asserting, judging, and so on, that these themselves have polar opposites. Opposition lies wholly on the side of what is believed, asserted or judged. Just as you can see a colour which is the opposite of another colour, but there is no such thing as *un*seeing a colour, there is nothing you can do to a colour which is the opposite of seeing it: so also men can think contrary thoughts, but there is no contrariety on the side of thinking, no such activity as *un*-thinking.

I do not think the same does go for desire; I think that the difference between desire and aversion is not adequately des-

[1]*In Reason and Argument* (Blackwell, 1976), p. 12.

cribable as the difference between desiring that p and desiring that not-p. If I am right, this again would show that the intentionality on the side of desire is different from the intentionality on the side of cogitation (to use McTaggart's term). There used to be a song about 'Accentuate the positive, eliminate the negative'; and I think one can distinguish among volitional and emotional attitudes between those that are positive: desire, love, joy, etc. and attitudes that are negative: aversion, fear, misery, anger, etc. Clearly someone whose attitudes are (in this sense) predominantly 'positive' will be happy, someone whose attitudes are in this sense predominantly 'negative' will be miserable. This is merely a psychological observation, not at all an acceptance of the precept of the song; I do not deny that the happiness of the man with positive attitudes may be a fool's paradise. I think that in this way again there is a difference between the intentionality of volitions and emotions and the intentionality of cogitations, namely, that there is this opposition between positive and negative attitudes on one side of our mental life, but not on the other. McTaggart admitted polar opposition for emotions and for pleasure and pain, but denied it for desire. Clearly he was right in what he admitted: hate is not love of an object opposite to the object of hate, nor is pain at some circumstance a pleasurable cogitation of the opposite circumstance; but I think he was wrong in explaining away aversion as desire for a negative state of affairs, and that the analogy he drew with disbelief and belief fails to hold.

9 Determining correspondence

In discussing matter, we saw how McTaggart deduces a contradiction concerning the existence of matter by using three premises: (i) the principle of sufficient description; (ii) the principle that every substance has parts, and thus has parts within parts *ad infinitum*; (iii) the principle of ontological determinacy. We must now see how McTaggart applies these principles to persons and their states. He holds that here the three principles can all be satisfied without contradiction, but only on certain conditions: only if the content of persons is of a certain very specific sort, quite different from the content they apparently have in present experience. But like Sherlock Holmes he concludes that when we have eliminated the impossible, whatever remains, however improbable it may seem, must be true.

The unreality of time comes in as a further condition for an acceptable solution. All the content of a given person must form one system of coexistent states. As we saw, McTaggart holds that the states of a person are one and all cogitations: if he has desires and emotions and pleasure and pain, these are colourings superadded to cogitations, not separate pieces of mental content. So let us first consider whether a system of simultaneous perceptions within a person could constitute an internal structure that satisfied our three principles.

Since we shall have much to say about perception in the rest of this book, it will be well to introduce here a small correction of McTaggart's terminology. He will say not only that a person G perceives H as being XYZ, but that G's perception of H perceives H as being XYZ. It will be clearer to say that this perception *represents* H as being XYZ.

As we saw, McTaggart holds (as Hume had already held) that a perception is differentiated in accordance with the way it represents the perceived object as being differentiated. It is only the *apparent* differentiation that counts: if a thing *has* parts, but these are not *perceived as* parts of it, the parts' merely being there does not differentiate a perception that represents the whole to which they belong. So a perception can be differentiated into parts within parts *ad infinitum* only if it represents its object as being differentiated into parts within parts *ad infinitum*.

This perception must moreover actually discriminate all these parts. For, parallel to the principle of ontological determinacy that we have already stated, McTaggart has also a principle of perceptual determinacy. I can form a judgement or assumption that the first Bishop of Rome had coloured irises in his eyes without any thought of what colour they had; but someone who had seen St Peter would have seen his irises as having some definite, absolutely determinate, colour – regardless of whether the percipient's colour-vision was perfect or not, and of whether he had any *name* for this definite colour. Again, if my myopic eyes do not let me tell whether what sits on yonder roof is a cat or a crow, all the same I see a black shape; and according to McTaggart my visual perception represents this as a perfectly determinate shape, whether I can conceptually grasp this exact shape or not.

Like the principle of ontological determinacy, the principle of perceptual determinacy is to be found in Berkeley and Hume (they, to be sure, did not clearly distinguish the two principles) and in many other philosophers. (Recently it has come in for some attack: there is the notorious problem whether if I see a hen as speckled I must see it has having a definite number of speckles – and whether I must 'see' a determinate number of stars if made to 'see stars' through a blow on the head!) It is not *derivable* from the principle of ontological determinacy: that my perception represents things with a certain measure of fuzziness might be included, or so it seems, in a fully determinate description of my perceptual state. Moreover, the principle appears hard to reconcile with the extensive appeal to confused perceptions that McTaggart, like Leibniz, has to make in order to save the appearances of our present life; though I am pretty sure he would have had an ingenious and plausible solution to the

E

difficulty if it had been raised. For the moment we must merely notice that this principle is a premise he treats as self-evident.

It follows that in order to *be* infinitely differentiated, a person's perception cannot even *represent* the perceived objects as matter divided *ad infinitum* in the spatio-temporal dimensions. For the trouble about matter was precisely that it would have to have more and more specific descriptions for finer and finer differentiation into parts, without there being any limit or last term of the series giving a completely determinate description, and this violates the principle of *ontological* determinacy. But similarly the impossibility in principle of such a completely determinate description for even the finest parts of matter would mean that there could not even *appear* to anyone's perception to be a material whole infinitely differentiated into parts: the principle of *perceptual* determinacy would be violated. A percipient thus cannot have an infinitely differentiated state of perception by perceiving things with material characteristics: what he perceives must be, and appear to be, of spiritual nature and itself infinitely differentiated. (Sense-data come in for no special consideration here: the notion of our perceiving sense-data is, I have argued, anyhow alien to McTaggart's system, and moreover sense-data are supposed to have merely some selection of the familiar characteristics of material bodies.)

A person *A* clearly cannot come to have an infinitely differentiated state of perception by perceiving such an infinitely differentiated state merely *within* himself. On this account, McTaggart regards solipsism as impossible. He would also regard this as one good reason for rejecting the belief in a freely creative God who is a solitary person; for such a God, had he freely chosen not to create, could with truth have been a solipsist. McTaggart, as we saw, believed that Christian belief affirms the existence of such a God, who can 'live and love alone'; but in this he was mistaken.

If *A*'s internal differentiation depends on perceiving differentiation *ad infinitum* within another person *B*, and *B* similarly depends for his internal differentiation upon perception of a third person *C*, and so on endlessly, we plainly have a vicious infinite regress. But if this series runs in a circle instead, do we not get a vicious circle? The winning move in McTaggart's intricate game is his realization that this need not be a vicious circle. We see this clearly if we assume a mini-society of just two persons, each of whom perceives each of the two clearly and distinctly, so that all the inner states of either are represented both to himself and to the other. A's content, on this hypothesis, will consist simply of A's perception of A and A's perception of B, and B's content will consist simply of B's perception of A and B's perception of B. Since the perception is entirely clear and distinct, each of these perceptions will have further parts: B's perception of A, for example, will have as parts B's perception of A's perception of B and B's perception of A's perception of A; and B's perceptions of A's perception of B's perception of A and of A's perception of B's perception of B will in turn be perceptions together making up B's perception of A's perception of B. This inner differentiation of A and B into perceptions can be worked out indefinitely; it is clear that McTaggart can satisfy the principle of infinite differentiation.

These parts within parts must all have sufficient descriptions. This condition is easily fulfillable, so long as we have sufficient descriptions of A and B to start with, if we impose one further condition. Let us suppose that all the perceptions with which we are presently concerned have a common characteristic, to which I shall for the moment refer simply as the characteristic of being d.c. perceptions. (The inwardness of these initials will be explained in a moment.) Let us further suppose that there is at most one d.c. perception *by* a given person *of* a given perceived object. Then e.g. 'A's d.c. perception of B's d.c. perception of A' will be an exclusive description of a perception; and if we supplant the proper names here used by sufficient descriptions of A and B, we shall have the perception in question sufficiently described. McTaggart uses the notation '$A!\ldots$', '$B!\ldots$' etc. to be short for 'A's (B's) d.c. perception of $\ldots$': it is then easy to work out what e.g. '$A!B!A!A!B$' stands for.

It remains for McTaggart to convince that the principles of ontological and perceptual determinacy are satisfied. The former principle will be satisfied because we do not get the same obstacle as we do for matter. There the trouble was that if at some stage of division each part is completely characterized e.g. in respect of colour, then each part will be homogeneous in colour, and *its* parts not distinguishable in colour; whereas if at each stage the parts have a variegated colour, which can be specified more clearly only by going down to *the parts of* those parts, then we have an endless series of more and more specific colour-characterizations, contrary to the principle of ontological determinacy. But with the d.c. system of mutually reflecting perceptions, we can work out descriptions of parts of perceptions (these will again be d.c. perceptions) in as much detail as we wish, all from the original specifications about who has d.c. perceptions of whom; we need not introduce any new specifications for a stage of more detailed differentiation. In fact McTaggart, to make this doubly sure, stipulates that after a finite number of stages of differentiation, *all* characteristics of more minutely differentiated d.c. perceptions shall be such as follow from description of the perceptions whose parts they are; this stipulation, even if not strictly necessary, appears perfectly possible, and would firmly guarantee that the principle of ontological determinacy is satisfied (418).

The principle of perceptual determinacy can also be satisfied, provided that the d.c. perceptions *represent* the persons and d.c. perceptions as forming a d.c. system. And it appears impossible that they should do otherwise; for, as we saw, a perception can *be* differentiated into parts only in so far as it *represents* its object *as* differentiated into parts; it can therefore *be* infinitely differentiated into parts only in so far as it *represents* its object as infinitely differentiated into parts. But the only way we have found for there to *be* infinite differentiation is for there to be persons with a d.c. system of mutual perceptions: so there cannot be a fully determinate *appearance* of infinite differentiation that will satisfy the principle of *perceptual* determinacy, unless the perceived objects are *represented* as forming a fully determinate d.c. system of persons and perceptions.

Obviously there is no need for this to happen with just *two* persons perceiving themselves and one another; it could easily be worked out e.g. that if A perceived A and B, B perceived B and C, and C perceived C and A, we could equally have the required system of d.c. perceptions. McTaggart spells out in some detail the many varieties of mutual perceptions that could be fitted into his general scheme.

The system of mutual perceptions that has here been sketched is called by McTaggart the Determining Correspondence system. McTaggart was not always happy in devising terminology, and here we have a term that does not remotely suggest the reality it is supposed to stand for. Gilbert Ryle at the end of his life protested at the growing fashion among philosophers to refer to theses, arguments, etc. by initials (e.g. 'TMA' for 'Third Man argument', 'R A A' for '*reductio ad absurdum*'), and in general I agree with his protest. I have, however, allowed myself to use 'd.c.' instead of 'determining correspondence', because here the phrase these initials abbreviate is no more illuminating or suggestive than they are.

According to McTaggart's account of imaging, a person *A* could have a differentiation into parts within parts to infinity if he *imaged* instead of *perceiving* an infinitely differentiated d.c. system of perceptions or imagings: for imagings are differentiated according to the parts of the imaginata, the objects imaged, just as perceptions are according to the parts of the percepta. Thus imaging raises no difficulties about how the parts within parts to infinity of a state of imaging could be constituted. McTaggart holds that we can 'image' a thing as having parts only in so far as we have imagings of the parts that together make up the imaging of the whole. But, as we also saw, Mc-Taggart decides against the reality of imagings on other grounds: namely, he argues that if I seem to image something I am really perceiving it, but misperceiving my own perception as a mere imaging. McTaggart's argument, we found, is very doubtful: it seems to involve an error in the logic of intentional constructions. If however he was right in denying the reality of imagings, his present conclusion must follow.

For judgements and assumptions McTaggart is on firmer ground: the infinitely differentiated structure within each person that can be generated by the person's mutual perception could not possibly be generated by their framing judgements or assumptions about one another. As we saw, a judgement or assumption would be internally differentiated, not in accordance with the parts of the object one was thinking about, but rather in a way *roughly* corresponding to the syntactical division of a sentence expressing the judgement or assumption. An act of judgement corresponding to the sentence 'Scissors cut paper' would have thought-constituents, such as I called Ideas in my book *Mental Acts*, corresponding to the words 'scissors' and 'paper', even though to the third word 'cut' there were to correspond rather a relation binding the two Ideas together, not a third Idea. But it would be ridiculous to suppose that this judgement had two parts corresponding to the two blades of the scissors! Even if I judge that A is made up of two parts B and C, my judgement does not then consist of two related judgements, one about B and one about C. Still less can we describe how if two persons made judgements about one another and about one another's judgements, this system of judgements could constitute a system of parts within parts to infinity. And the like applies to assumptions, whose internal structure is just like that of judgements. We need not dwell upon awarenesses of characteristics; for we saw reason to deny that these exist as distinct mental acts, rather than as mere aspects of judgement or assumptions, like my Ideas (420–1).

Let me now sum up. In the domain of persons we can provide for the simultaneous fulfilment of our three principles: sufficient description, ontological determinacy, and infinite differentiation. But this appears to be possible in only one way: the persons in question must have no content except their perceptions of themselves and one another; and the mutual perception must be absolutely clear and distinct, so that the infinitely complex differentiation of perceptions within any person A is fully mirrored in A's introspective perception of A and in any perception of A by a person B.

This system of perceptions, the d.c. perceptions, must form the complete content of any person A. Thus A's whole mental life must consist of perceptions. This, as I have said, does not exclude the perceptions' being appetitively or emotionally coloured, or pleasurable or painful. But it does require that in any person who has d.c. perceptions there is no discursive thought to contrast with the intuitive experience of perception. Broad indeed suggests that though no single perception could be a discursive thought, perhaps several perceptions somehow combined together could be; but I find this suggestion unintelligible, and cannot but regard McTaggart as having thought consequently when he denied that any person totally differentiated into a system of d.c. perceptions could also have discursive thoughts.

Of the characteristics empirically given, McTaggart has argued that time is delusory and that objects possessing only material characteristics could not satisfy the three ontological principles we have been discussing. There remains spirit: that is to say, there remain persons, for McTaggart holds that any experience belongs of necessity to some person (and cannot also be another's experience). Persons can satisfy the requirements, but only if each person's content is wholly made up of a d.c. system of perceptions: and the persons and their d.c. perceptions must be timeless. Whether the d.c. perceptions not only *are* timeless, but also *represent* persons and d.c. perceptions as timeless, we have not yet determined: we shall later consider McTaggart's reasons for an affirmative answer.

McTaggart came to believe that the reality of the Universe is a system of persons, perceiving themselves and one another clearly and distinctly, long before he worked out the elaborate arguments for this conclusion that we find in *The Nature of Existence*. We find it already stated in *Some Dogmas of Religion* and in McTaggart's Hegelian writings. In his Hegelian period McTaggart decided that the concrete filling-out of the abstract category that Hegel called 'the absolute idea' could be nothing but such a system of persons; whether he was here a faithful Hegelian I shall not inquire. Having decided that Hegel's logic was an unsound method, McTaggart undauntedly set to work devising a new proof, with apparatus of logic and analysis accessible to his Cambridge contemporaries, as Hegelian dialectic had not been. As I have remarked, he was utterly convinced that his mystical experience (he called it 'the *Saul* feeling'[1]) was a true vision; and he laboured to get over the content of the

[1] By allusion to Robert Browning's poem *Saul.*

vision to others by way of discursive thought, which alone could convince those who lacked the vision itself. Like Aquinas, he believed firmly that truth could not contradict truth and that the ultimate reality, however wonderful, could not be contra-rational; with sufficient skill and patience (and he had abund-ance of both) the riddle must be rationally soluble so as to yield what he already knew was the right answer.

In presenting the doctrine of determining correspondence, I have run together chapters in the first volume of *The Nature of Existence*, where the doctrine is presented in a rebarbatively abstract form, and chapters in the second volume that clothe the dry bones with flesh. This makes the theory much easier to grasp, and does not, I think, distort it. As I mentioned in the chapter on Matter, my presentation does involve a considerable departure from McTaggart's theory of metaphysical method; but that methodology is a grave liability; assuming the role of counsel for McTaggart, I have here omitted to put in pleadings that would only weaken the case.

Since only persons with a d.c. system of perceptions can satisfy McTaggart's *a priori* principles, he concludes that only such persons exist and that their whole inner experience is of the nature of perception, not discursive thought. The hardihood of a thinker who thought he had no thoughts, judged that he made no judgements, and inferred that he drew no inferences, needs no comment. We shall see in the next chapter that Mc-Taggart had a good defence against the charge that at this point his system becomes flatly self-contradictory; it remains true that the conclusion is extremely unplausible.

In present experience we do perceive persons as persons; here for once McTaggart's view does not depart from common sense, and we need not here consider the philosophical arguments to show the contrary to be the case. But we perceive persons as having material, sensible, characteristics, and there appears on the face of it no inconsistency between these characteristics and personality. McTaggart is going to argue, however, that this too is a delusion; material characteristics are incompatible with personality and any perception representing a person as having them is thus far misrepresentation.

McTaggart's argument has two premises: first, that persons are differentiated into mental states, that mental states form the whole content of persons; second, that no mental states have any material or sensible characteristics. We had some considerations about the first premise in the last chapter. The second premise is now expressly denied by a powerful school of contemporary philosophers, the central state materialists, who say that a mental state is nothing other than a certain perturbation of the brain. There are those among them who think that the use of mental terminology is a superstition, like talk of the Devil or of witchcraft, and look forward to a day when human vocabulary has been improved in this respect. I need not dwell upon people who, like McTaggart, are trying to think they have no thoughts, but unlike him do not think they even have other mental states that could be mistaken for thoughts. I shall confine myself to the more reasonable view that mental states combine mental and physical (physiological) characteristics: it was this view that McTaggart considered and rejected.

One argument we often meet with nowadays goes like this. There is overwhelming evidence that each sort of mental state is correlated with a particular sort of brain-change or brain-state; whenever that sort of thing goes on in a brain, the man whose brain it is is in a certain mental state. Now if the mental states thus one-sidedly dependent on brain conditions are nevertheless different entities, we shall have an undesirable proliferation of kinds of entities, and many of these entities will be 'nomological danglers'. It would be better to apply Ockham's razor and say that the mental states simply *are* the brain states they are commonly supposed to depend on.

I need not consider anything about this argument except its first premise. It is simply bluff on the part of people who use the argument when they talk of 'overwhelming evidence'. An honest physiologist will admit that very little is known even of the processes in a parrot's brain when a parrot 'talks'; confident claims to know *which* brain processes account for the rational talk of a man are impudent charlatanism.

However, the reason I should offer for rejecting the view that a given state of mind is identical with a given state of the brain is not the weakness of the argument in its favour, but simply that I find it not coherently graspable. Some of the central state materialists think they have given a strict account of what they mean when they say 'identical' just by prefixing the adverb 'strictly' to 'identical'; but they deceive themselves.

Imagine some philosopher who tried to revive Pythagoreanism (and I do not think it is safe to say that any old error is quite beyond revival). Suppose he were to say, as the Pythagoreans did, that the virtue of justice is the number four. 'How do you mean "is"?' I might ask. 'I mean,' says the Pythagorean, 'that justice is none other than the number four: they are strictly identical. Of course I recognize that the arithmetical characteristics commonly ascribed to the number four are quite different from the ethical characteristics commonly ascribed to the virtue of justice. But my thesis is that there is one single eternal object that has both sets of characteristics.' Do I now understand his thesis any better? Certainly not. And I am equally at a loss if a central state materialist assures me that some cerebral disturbance of mine simply *is*, is strictly identical with, my sudden recollection that I must go to the Bank.

McTaggart's second premise, that mental and physiological characteristics of states simply will not fit together, is thus very reasonable indeed. And I think there is also some true sense for the first premise: that a person is fully comprised in his various mental states, that they are all there is to him. Must we then draw McTaggart's conclusion: that persons are wholly immaterial, that their apparent sensible characteristics are delusory? I do not think so. The hinge on which the argument turns is strengthless: we have here a great weakness in McTaggart's philosophy, to which I have already adverted, his assumption that such terms as 'part', 'whole', 'content', etc. are univocal. Because of this he would suppose that if a person's content or make-up at a given time can be given *both* by saying what organs he has under his hide *and* by saying what thoughts and feelings he has, then this is like giving the make-up of England now by listing the ecclesiastical dioceses and now by listing the counties. England is made up both ways, but of course this is because the dioceses and the counties overlap, have common parts; so if I have a mental make-up and a physiological make-up, something must be e.g. both a bit of a brain-cell and a part of a mental state. This however would follow from the two premises only if 'whole', 'part', etc. were univocal terms; I have said that I doubt this, and thus I feel at liberty to accept McTaggart's two premises and reject his immaterialist conclusion.

Let us now summarize what McTaggart's results are supposed to be at this stage. He claims to have rigorously proved that there is no time, and that there cannot be anything whose *sole* attributes are some or all of the characteristics humanly attributed to matter (this, as we have seen, would also rule out the philosophers' sense-data). There can however be spirit; indeed, there *must* be spirit, for if anything even appears to exist there is an appearance which is a state of some person. If the argument we have just considered were a valid argument with true premises, we could further conclude that spirit cannot ever have any of the characteristics of matter. Since we have no concrete descriptions to fill up the abstract schematic concept of a substance, except ones of either material or mental characteristics, we have not the least reason to think there is any individual that is neither spiritual nor material; so, McTaggart concludes, we may reasonably hold that spirit, differentiated into individual persons, alone exists, and that persons' appearing to have material characteristics is an illusion.

As we have seen, McTaggart thinks he can show that the contradiction which ruled out the existence of matter can be avoided for spirit only if spirits have the sort of mutual clear and distinct perception that McTaggart calls determining correspondence. McTaggart accordingly claims (using the legal formula 'I submit') that the theory of determining correspondence has been proved.

10   Error

If McTaggart's earlier conclusions can be accepted, there will be enormous differences between our *prima facie* view of the Universe and the absolute reality. It will not be just a matter of philosophy's requiring the rejection of judgements commonly accepted; much of our perception will have been shown by philosophy to be misperception, misrepresentation of the objects perceived.

The main varieties of error that McTaggart's metaphysics require to exist may be described as follows (505: for reasons already stated, I have cut out McTaggart's confusing references to sense-data):

1   McTaggart claims to have proved that no reality can be temporal or changeable. But he also holds that in present experience *all* perceptions represent their objects as temporal and as changing with time; we shall see presently how he deals with certain apparent exceptions. This is the most pervasive and fundamental form of error.

2   In present experience most of what we perceive appears to have the geometrical and extensible characteristics of matter. But according to McTaggart it involves a positive contradiction that any reality should have *only* those material characteristics. The only other kind of individual reality in our acquaintance is spirit; it is therefore reasonable to believe that spirit alone exists. But there is a synthetic incompatibility between the real characteristics of spirit and what would be the characteristics of matter if matter existed. So we must conclude that what we perceive is all really spirit – all constituted by persons and their mental states and acts – and when it seems in part to have any of the characteristic traits of matter it is being misperceived.

3 In introspection each of us perceives himself as having states of mind that are not perceptions, but judgements, assumptions, or imagings. But in reality there are no states of mind except perceptions (though these may be variously coloured with desire or emotion).

4 Spirit can have the actually complete and fully determinate internal differentiation required by McTaggart's principles only if there exists a d.c. system of perception: each person P must perceive a certain group G of persons, possibly including himself, and must perceive all the perceptions of each person in group G, so that we get an infinitely finely differentiated system of perceptions. Not only so, but further, all the perceptions by persons in the group G must *appear* to the percipient P as a d.c. system; for only thus, McTaggart argues, could P's own perceptions *be* so differentiated as to form a d.c. system. But whatever we perceive in present experience, either inside ourselves or outside ourselves, is perceived as only finitely differentiated, and assuredly as not forming anything remotely like a d.c. system.

There must, then, be very much error in the world; and for McTaggart all this error must be misperception, since there are no judgements to be false: the appearance of there being such acts of the mind as judgements will itself be introspective misperception. However, it is not an error that there is such a thing as error. Absurd as the contrary thesis appears, some thinkers appear committed to it: both in Parmenides and in Mrs Eddy (and surely it must have been her inheritance from Parmenides, by way of some mirky popularized Transcendentalism, that phrase 'the error of mortal mind'!) you get the impression that mortal mind is an error erroneously representing itself to exist. McTaggart has not painted himself into the corner like this. As he shows (510), to say it is only an error that there is any error is self-contradictory.

Some unfriendly readers might ask whether McTaggart is not after all quite as badly off as Parmenides and Mrs Eddy, since he must judge that there is no such thing as judgement and go on to infer that there is no such thing as inference. McTaggart looked this difficulty firmly in the eye, but unlike the legendary Scottish minister, did not pass it by. He denied the parity of reasoning. If one were to say that there is only an appearance of error, the very appearance must then itself be an error. But an introspective appearance that I am judging something need not even present itself as a *judgement* that a judgement is being made; and even if there does appear to be a judgement that I am judging, this again does not logically require that there should actually be a judgement about judgement. Similarly, and even more clearly, for inference: for the introspective appearance of there being an inference will normally not present itself as an *inference* that there is an inference going on. It would indeed be quite suicidal for McTaggart to deny the things that we appear to know discursively, by judgement and inference; but he is not doing this, he is only denying that our knowledge really is, as it appears to be, discursive.

How scandalous is the amount of error that McTaggart requires should exist? It is certainly not contrary even to common sense that there should be misperception, even a lot of misperception. As regards the delusion that McTaggart accounts as fundamental, the delusion of time, quite ordinary people may find themselves bewildered when they think about time: worries about the reality of time do not require a peculiar academic discipline of first learning to worry and then learning to get rid of your worries; they appear to be part of the human condition. Remember the two elderly working men (page 22) who argued in a pub about whether tomorrow ever comes. In this sort of bewilderment, the solution that time can only be a delusive appearance may not seem utterly unacceptable.

Similarly for our perception of matter. It is mere common sense to allow that in detail our perceptions of material objects are to some extent mistaken; and even to allow for certain systematic misperceptions – e.g. as regards the size of distant objects. Sense-datum philosophers often refer to a position called Naïve Realism, according to which all sense-perception is correct and objects just are as they appear to the senses. But it would be very hard to find anyone who really held this doctrine – though the Epicureans, who held that the sun and moon are only as big as they look, perhaps came near to doing so; and a naïve realist would need to be a sophisticated philosopher to maintain his position against the attacks of science and common sense. A man of common sense who has picked up a little science may even suppose (I do not say: rightly suppose) that certain entire genera of perceived characteristics are delusive. He may e.g. suppose that though we perceive things as coloured, things in themselves are not coloured: it is not merely that we do not always see the right colour of a thing, a thing has not in itself got any colour.

Even as regards introspection, since Freud's work many people would be willing to admit that our introspective account of what goes on in our own minds may contain a good deal of suppression and distortion. This part of McTaggart's theory of error is however the part that many will find altogether incredible. In his book *Idealism*, Dr Ewing has used the simile that without knowing how many cups of tea a day one could drink without peril to health, one can say a thousand cups a day would certainly be too many: he argues that the kind and degree of introspective error affirmed by McTaggart is as certainly known to be too much. It is hard not to agree.

We must here observe how impossible it becomes to understand McTaggart's theory of misperception if we follow Broad and replace 'perception' throughout by the Cambridge philosophers' term of art, 'prehension'. This term was introduced for the way a person is supposed to cognize his own sense-data. Since sense-data should really possess the characteristics (or some of them) that material objects appear to our senses as possessing, distinguishing between the appearance and the reality of sense-data themselves would deprive sense-data of their theoretical role; it was thus natural for the sense-datum philosophers in McTaggart's Cambridge to regard prehension of sense-data as wholly correct. But I have already argued that sense-data have no proper place in McTaggart's philosophy; neither is there any place for prehension, as opposed to perception. It would of course be unintelligible how prehension could err; but it is only because he has accustomed himself to saying 'prehension' instead of 'perception' that Broad finds himself completely baffled by the doctrine that perception can err.

What then can McTaggart mean when he says (e.g. in 513) that all perception is 'self-evidently' correct? If he were using the adverb to refer to a self-evident truth, he would be flatly contradicting himself: for on his view it is not even true, let alone self-evidently true, that every perception is correct. But it is easy to restore consistency by amending McTaggart's language; we need only borrow some legal jargon that has recently become current in philosophy, which would surely have been to the taste of the Absolute's shrewd family solicitor.[1] Perception, we may say, has of its nature a *presumptive* correctness. If this were not so, then as McTaggart argues (513) we should be lost in almost complete scepticism. But the presumption of correctness is a *defeasible* presumption; it stands until actually defeated, but it *can* be defeated.

The presumption of correctness is for McTaggart closely bound up with the appearances of time; for the natural words to express the presumption in a particular case are: 'This that I perceive is as I perceive it *while I now perceive it.*' There is no general presumption that this that I perceive is as I perceive it before or after I perceive it. Obviously for McTaggart the proposition expressing the presumptive accuracy of a perception cannot as it stands be even true, let alone self-evidently true, for its literal truth would require the reality of time. To get something that can actually be true, we need an amended form of words:

This that I perceive is as I perceive it, subject to the condition of my perceiving this in a *C* series, certain terms of which are apparent in my perception as a specious present.

(Remember that the *C* series is that real series whose terms and their order underlie the appearance of events occurring in a temporal order.) McTaggart holds that the amended form really is a self-evident proposition; but now it no longer guarantees that perceptions do not err. For the proviso that replaces 'which

---

[1] I owe this sobriquet for McTaggart to Broad; it aptly describes the lawyer-like care and clarity of McTaggart's arguments.

I now perceive it' positively requires some error; it requires at least the delusion of time, and from this delusion, as we shall see, others follow (514, 515, 591).

Suppose that the perception P represented its object, not as being in a specious present, nor yet as past or future, but as being what it really is – eternally existent. In that case the proviso restricting the guarantee that perception P is correct would vanish, and P would be unconditionally correct. Perception free from the delusion of time is free from all delusions (515, 552).

Are there in present experience any perceptions that are free from the delusion of time? Do we ever break completely through the veil of Maya and see the world as it timelessly is? Mystics have often claimed this; McTaggart was temperamentally drawn to mysticism, but he would not admit the claim. On the contrary, he firmly asserted that in present experience *all* perceptions are infected at least with the delusion of time (516, 525). This shows his extreme intellectual probity. Highly as he valued his own mystical experiences, which must psychologically speaking have done much to strengthen his convictions as to the nature of the Universe, he strictly abstained from appealing to them as evidence for others, and even from counselling others to seek such experiences. Mystical experience could at best be less delusive than vulgar experience; wholly correct it could not be, since even here we do not overcome the delusion of time. For Spinoza the eyes of the mind, by which we perceive and experience our own eternity, are none other than proofs (*Ethics*, V.23, *scholium*); and so it was for McTaggart also. (To be sure, what in present experience we seem to grasp only inferentially by proofs, we really know by direct perception; the appearance that much of our knowledge is only discursive is itself a delusion of present experience. We shall see later how McTaggart avoids self-contradiction at this point.)

The theoretical grounds for denying that in mystical experience an object is apprehended as being eternal were indeed very strong. For when a perception is itself perceived, it is always perceived as being in time. And an 'apparent perception' – a perception that is not only perceived, but perceived *as* a perception – always appears as standing in a time-relation to its object, namely the near-simultaneity of the specious present; this comes out in the words naturally used to express the *prima facie* guarantee of the perception's correctness – 'while I now perceive'. So if I perceive a perception *P* of an object *O*, and perceive *P* *as* a perception of *O*, then I perceive *O* as standing in a time-relation to *P*; and therefore not as timeless, since *P* is not perceived as timeless (524).

Some writers on mysticism (e.g. Aldous Huxley) have claimed that the mystical experience itself, as well as its object, appears as eternal. McTaggart rightly dismisses this claim as a confusion of thought. *Sub specie temporis*, there is a point of time at which the mystical experience has not yet begun, and a later point by when it has ceased. To admit this and yet deny that the experience appears to have a place in the time series is mere confusion. Such experiences 'are usually states of high excitement, and always of intense contemplation, and, while they continue, the lapse of time is not noticed, nor, when they are over, is it easy to judge how much time has elapsed'. But this is no good reason to say that the experience does not appear to happen in time, or to doubt the universality of temporal appearance in this life (524–5).

But can't we show in another way, on McTaggart's own premises, that some present experiences must be free from the delusion of time? Consider McTaggart's own apparent judgement, 'I am eternal.' In reality this will not be a judgement, but a perception introspectively misperceived as a judgement; so must not the state which McTaggart misperceived as this judgement have been, on his own showing, a *perception* of himself as being eternal? McTaggart had an answer to the objection, which is one he himself raised; it is not a mere *adhocus-pocus*, but a natural result of a general view about introspective appearances, a view worked out in considerable detail (630–88).

McTaggart makes no attempt to explain in detail the misperception of things as material. No doubt he was warned off these rocks and shoals by the disastrous shipwreck of Hegel's *Philosophy of Nature*; he read the work conscientiously through, but remarked, 'What rot it is!' Science had made enormous progress since Hegel's days, and McTaggart will have despaired of digesting the accumulated data so as to give even an outline account of sensory phenomena. In 368 there is a hint that he thought the phenomena of geometrical perspective were explicable in his idealistic system. (Notice that he here speaks of misperceiving spiritual entities as *moving bodies*, and does not bring sense-data into the account, even though they figure in the text of Broad that McTaggart is here criticizing. This is one more indication of what an alien growth the sense-datum theory is in McTaggart's system.) But the theory remains a sketch: and we may be glad that McTaggart did not waste his energies in philosophy of nature.

The phenomenology of mind, on the other hand, is worked out in great detail, and with great subtlety and rigour. The starting-point is that the general theory positively requires that not all perceptions in present experience can be 'apparent perceptions' – perceptions introspectively appearing as perceptions. For clearly we apprehend objects at various stages of the C series – not only in the specious present, but in the apparent past and future as well. For McTaggart, our cogitations of these objects will be perceptions: in my apprehension of the 'past' and 'future' I shall in fact be perceiving some things *as* past and other things *as* future. But I cannot have *apparent* perceptions of objects as being past or future: if my perception P represents its object O as past or future, P itself cannot be perceived as a perception. For if P itself did introspectively appear as a perception, and as representing a past or future object, then the *prima facie* guarantee of P's correctness would take the form 'O was as I perceive it which I now perceive it' or 'O will be as I perceive it while I now perceive it'. But these forms contain inconsistent time-specifications and are quite absurd. Thus a perception which represents its object as past or future will itself be introspectively represented not as a perception but as a cogitation of some other kind – a judgement, assumption, or imaging (634, 674).

The misperception of a perception as a judgement has two essential features. First, only *part* of what is given in perception appears as the information given in this judgement: that is why we seem to have wholly true or wholly false judgements, although the perception which appears under the guise of judgement really represents some features of its object correctly and others erroneously (640, 644, 660). Second, the internal structure of the perception is misperceived. *Prima facie*, as we saw, a judgement appears to be differentiated, to have structure, not in accordance with the parts of the object that is being judged about, but rather in accordance with the *words* in which the judgement would be expressed (421); the judgement expressed by, 'The fat cat sat on the mat' might have elements corresponding to 'fat', 'cat', and 'mat', but would certainly not correspond in structure to the anatomy of the fat cat. These apparent elements of judgement would be what McTaggart calls awarenesses of characteristics (672); there is no reason to suppose – as he perhaps did – that there even *appears* in introspection to be an awareness of a characteristic outside the context of an act of judging or assuming. McTaggart holds that the fundamental error by which a perception appears as a judgement consists in this: the introspecting person takes the presentation of many characteristics in one perceptual act to be a differentiation of the act itself into elements corresponding to the characteristics (661).[1]

Among the things given in perception, as we saw, are the characteristics *of* perceived characteristics – we can *see* colours as incompatible, or the like. McTaggart appeals to this to explain judgements of general and abstract kinds: to use his own example, the judgement that no poet can be an aeroplane may be the guise in which introspection represents a perception of Smith as being-a-poet-which-involves-not-being-an-aeroplane, where the hyphenation shows that all this is given in one perceptual act (684). And this same machinery is used to explain how I can simultaneously (as it seems) perceive A as being X and judge that A cannot be X; for McTaggart, there is just *one* act of perception, in which I perceive A as X but also as being-

---

[1] In giving this exposition, I have supposed that McTaggart sometimes slipped into writing 'characteristics' when he meant 'awarenesses of characteristics'. This is the sort of slip one expects to find in a work whose author could not give it a final revision. Broad triumphs about yet another confusion exposed!

Z-which-excludes-being-X; but by a sort of introspective double vision I seem to myself to have *two* states – a perception of A as X, a judgement that A is not X. And here we find his explanation how a man can make an apparent judgement that things are not in time, although this judgement is really a perception which, like all in our present life, represents its object as temporal; we need only read 'X' above as 'temporal'. However unplausible this account may be, we see that judgements denying temporality are not dealt with *ad hoc*, but under a wide-ranging theory of judgement. And there is no sound objection to the theory on the score that it involves perceiving objects as having incompatible characteristics together; for Escher's engravings show us how we can see objects just like that – as combining incompatible characteristics.

I have no space to do justice to McTaggart's phenomenology of judgement; and I must pass over what he says about apparent inferences, assumptions and imagings. It is amusing to notice that he describes as 'wild and improbable' the idea that what appears as the act of assuming the sea to be boiling hot is really a misperception of something as being a boiling hot sea (671); and similarly, the idea that the act of imaging, mentally picturing, the execution of George III in Berkeley Square is really a misperception of some actual state of affairs as being such an execution (675). There were limits to the misperceptions that McTaggart was prepared to assume!

The key to the problem of error, and the final answer to the question whether *any* perception is free from delusion, in particular from the delusion of time, will be found in the account of the C series, which is misperceived as time-order. This is our next topic.

11 The *C* series

It is an unfortunate fact about the English language that a number of words ending in '-es' with a long vowel, like 'species' and 'series', have the same form in the plural. Lewis Carroll boldly wrote 'soriteses', which by classical standards is not less correct than 'sorites' (the Greek plural would be 'soritai'), and proposed that we say 'specieses' and 'serieses' too; but few will follow him. When McTaggart has 'the *C* series' in his text or in the titles of his chapters, should it be read as singular or as plural? Clearly, I think, as plural. A *C* series is what corresponds in reality to the appearance of a series of events in time; and so in each person there will be a distinct *C* series, which he misperceives as the temporal series of his own experiences.

We can apprehend the same object 'at different times'; this apprehension must really be perception, so in a given person there are perceptions of the very same object occurring at different stages of his *C* series. This means that the *C* series in a person *A* cannot be an ordering of *A*'s d.c. parts; in the d.c. system of perceptions this is just *one* perception of *A* by himself, *A !A*, but 'in the course of time', i.e. in the *C* series, *A* will have many perceptions of himself, quite different in character. So we have to introduce a new dimension of each person, at right angles so to speak to his differentiation into d.c. perceptions as parts, in order to find room within him for the varied misperceptions of our present experience. But since the d.c. perceptions exhaustively comprise the person whose states they are, it is at first difficult to see how there can be room in *A* for *other* perceptions of the same objects as are represented in the d.c. perceptions (539–40).

McTaggart's solution is to say that *A*'s d.c. perception of any given object, say of *A* himself or of *B* or of *B!A*, contains *within it* a whole set of 'fragmentary' perceptions of the very same object; since these fragmentary perceptions are only parts of the d.c. perceptions, their occurrence does not bring any new content to the person A that was not already supplied in A's d.c. perceptions (541–2).

We have already seen how the d.c. perceptions satisfy McTaggart's requirement that parts within parts to infinity shall have sufficient description without our having a problem with the principle of ontological determinacy – because all the details of the differentiation *ad infinitum* can be worked out once we know which persons are mirrored in the perceptions of each given person. But on the face of it our perceptions in present experience are not differentiated in this infinitely detailed way; they could be so only if they represented their objects as infinitely differentiated into parts within parts, and they do not do so.

McTaggart ingeniously overcomes this difficulty. He uses the symbols 'c_x', 'c_y', etc. to mean 'that fragmentary perception, at the stage x or y of the C series, which is part of –––––––', the blank being filled with a designation of some d.c. perception. Fragmentary perceptions, regardless of how they represent things, can thus all be supplied with sufficient descriptions; we need only add the part indicated by the symbol 'c_x' to the sufficient description of a d.c. part, say $A!B$, in order to get a sufficient description of the fragmentary part $c_xA!B$. The d.c. perceptions, as we saw, could all be distinguished from one another, in parts within parts *ad infinitum*, only if they were perfectly clear and distinct perceptions, in which there were distinctively represented parts within parts *ad infinitum* of the perceived objects. But no such requirement holds for fragmentary parts. Once the d.c. parts are individuated, fragmentary parts within parts *ad infinitum* at a given stage of the C series are individuated simply by which stage of the C series they are at and which d.c. perceptions they are fragmentary parts of. They need not, like the d.c. perceptions, be perfectly clear and distinct in order to be individuated; they may on the contrary be highly confused.

To explain confused perception further, McTaggart uses the

symbol ' + ' after the name of a substance to mean '. . . and all its d.c. parts'. The d.c. perceptions $A!(B+)$ will thus *both* be the system of d.c. perceptions that are parts of $A!B$, *and* be the perceptions of *all* the d.c. parts of B; but if we take a fragmentary perception, then $c_xA!(B+)$ need not be such an infinitely differentiated perception; we may have here only *one* perception, which represents B but fails to discriminate all, or even any, further parts within B. There will be an infinite system of fragmentary perceptions comprised within $c_xA!B$, but these will not represent their objects distinctly, they will all be completely confused (596–7).

Like Leibniz, then, McTaggart extensively uses the idea of confused perception. Like Leibniz again, he uses this idea to explain away the apparent fluctuation of a person A's perceptual field with time. At any stage of A's C series, McTaggart holds, the same range of perceived objects are represented; the field appears to fluctuate with time because some of it is only confusedly perceived and at different stages of the C series different parts of the field are confusedly perceived. Introspection, McTaggart remarks, already shows us that our clear and distinct perceptions have a vague background of confused perception; we cannot in principle get a better look at this vague background, for it is a psychological law that the more confused a perception is the more confused is the perceiver's introspective awareness of it (603–4; 808).

The delusion of time prevails in all our states of fragmentary perception; but McTaggart holds that the perceptions of the d.c. system are not only supremely clear and distinct but also exempt from the delusion of time. McTaggart has an intricate argument to prove this, one that extorts Broad's admiration (549–51).

Let us consider a typical d.c. perception, say $A!B!G$. If $A!B!G$ is to represent $B!G$, B's d.c. perception of G, as being in time, there are just three possibilities. (i) $A!B!G$ may represent $B!G$ as being in time without representing as temporal the fragmentary parts of $B!G$ in B's C series. (ii) $A!B!G$ may represent $B!G$ as occupying a time separate from the time occupied by the fragmentary perceptions within $B!G$. (iii) $A!B!G$ may represent

B!G as occupying a time within which the fragmentary states of *B*'s perception of *G* are to occur.

Alternatives (i) and (ii) may be quickly dismissed. If *A* in his d.c. perceptions has any cognizance of *B*'s fragmentary states of perception of *G*, *A* can have this only by reason of these states' being represented within *A*'s d.c. perception of *B!G*. For *B!G* is the whole, of which *B*'s fragmentary apprehensions of *G* will be parts; *A* then in his d.c. perceptions will thus discriminate these parts within *B!G* only if they are represented in *A*'s perception *A!B!G*. But *B!G* alone, as a single term, cannot be represented as temporal in *any* perception of *A*'s, unless *other* terms of *B*'s *C* series are *also* represented, and *B!G* seems to stand in a time-relation to these: and this excludes alternative (i). Again, if the fragmentary parts of *B!G* are represented in *A!B!G* as temporal, then of course *B!G* will be represented as lasting in time at least as long as the fragmentary parts of *B!G* appear to last; *B!G* cannot be represented as occupying a separate time from its fragmentary parts. This excludes alternative (ii).

The remaining alternative, (iii), is that the fragmentary parts of *B!G* should be represented in *A!B!G* as occupying times within the whole time occupied by *B!G*. Now as we saw in Chapter 9, *B!G* will be free from various forms of error. In the d.c. perceptions persons are represented as persons, perceptions as perceptions; there is no appearance of there being matter, or of there being non-perceptual states of mind like judgements and suppositions. And not only will e.g. the d.c. perception *B!G* itself *be* free from these errors; the d.c. perception *A!B!G* clearly and distinctly represents *B!G*, and will *represent* it as being free from these errors. But in a fragmentary state $c_x B!G$ *B* may well misperceive e.g. a person *G* as having material as well as spiritual characteristics. So if $c_x B!G$ is misrepresented in the d.c. perception *A!B!G* as occupying part of the temporal duration of *B!G*, *A* will be misperceiving *B* as *both* perceiving *G* correctly in certain respects for the whole of a period, *and* misperceiving *G* in those very respects for part of the period! This, McTaggart argues, is impossible; but it would be possible on our third alternative, so that also is excluded.

One result is that whether fragmentary parts like $c_x B!G$ are or are not discriminated in A's d.c. perception of $B!G$, $B!G$ itself will not be there represented as temporal. But if $A!B!G$ does not misrepresent $B!G$ itself as temporal, neither can any fragmentary states like $c_x B!G$ be perceived by A as temporal in the act of perceiving $B!G$: if the whole $B!G$ is being represented as non-temporal, any parts discriminated within $B!G$ in the act of perception $A!B!G$ will likewise be represented as non-temporal. Therefore the d.c. perceptions are wholly exempt from the great time-delusion; in these perceptions, neither persons, nor other d.c. perceptions, nor yet fragmentary states of perception, can be represented as temporal.

It follows again, by McTaggart's general theory of error, that the d.c. perceptions are free from any kind of error whatsoever. All perception has a *prima facie* presumption in its favour that it is correct; for McTaggart, as for any sensible man, the presumption is defeasible, there can be illusion or misperception; but McTaggart further holds that the *only* restriction upon the inerrancy of perception is one which *sub specie temporis* comes out as a temporal restriction ('This which I perceive is as I perceive it *while I now* perceive it') and in reality is a restriction of accuracy due to our perceiving under the false form of time. With that false form removed all perceptions are completely accurate; A need not perceive all the characteristics of the things he perceives, but he does not, in his d.c. perceptions, perceive anything as being what it is not (552).

Thus, though we really do misperceive things (we are not just under an illusion of being under illusions, as foolish oriental thinkers would have us believe), McTaggart holds that in each person there is a state of perception, the system of d.c. perceptions, which is exhaustive of the person's whole psychical content and which is wholly free from error; which not only *is* timeless, as all things must be if time is illusory, but is *self-consciously* eternal. This result is already much: that we should know that such error-free, self-consciously eternal perception not only exists in the Universe somewhere, but is actually available to each one of us. The emotional quality of this eternal life I shall discuss in the next chapter.

Since McTaggart is not going to deny or evade the existence

of error, can he give any account of how error comes about? The answer necessarily involves grave difficulties, and unfortunately it appears that, owing to the work's being incompletely revised, there is a mistake in McTaggart's exposition at the crucial point (579–80). For simplicity's sake I shall first comment on the text as I think it ought to read, and then try to justify my emendation.

McTaggart, in a footnote to 579, asks us to consider the whole perceptual state of a person, at a given stage of his C series as forming one single perception: such stages would be designated as c_xG, c_yG, etc. Similarly, the total content of G's d.c. perceptions is the content of the person G himself; let us for the moment, however, think of G as the totality of G's d.c. perception. McTaggart, by my reading of him, is arguing that the C stages c_xG, c_yG, etc. cannot *be* distinct states of perception from the total state of d.c. perception, G, unless they *misrepresent themselves* as each having content *separate* from the content of G (and from that of other C stages as well). It would follow, and does follow according to McTaggart (589), that in a person who had no self-perception this misrepresentation of C stages *in* the C stages themselves is impossible, and consequently there could be no C stages distinct from the d.c. perceptions.

The fragmentary states do not misrepresent themselves as being distinct states of perception, they really are distinct; but they could not, McTaggart thinks, *be* distinct unless they *misrepresented* their content as mutually exclusive. This must be misrepresentation, misperception, at least as regards the relation between c_xG and G, which so far from being excluded from c_xG wholly includes it; we shall see shortly that the mutual relation of c_xG and c_yG is also misrepresented in these states of perception. We need not go back on our view that the d.c. state of G is wholly inerrant: the states c_xG, c_yG, etc. are distinct from the d.c. perception of the same perceptual field by being states of more or less erroneous perception; and if *they* are distinct from the d.c. perception, *it* has no need to misrepresent itself in order to be distinct from *them* (580).

This is the reason why, if there are fragmentary states of perception in a person representing the same set of objects as the correct d.c. perceptions do, the fragmentary states must be states of misrepresentation. If c_xG, c_yG, c_zG, etc. are states of misperception, then by our previous argument they must misrepresent one another, and other objects of perception, as being temporal. And it indeed seems characteristic of temporal appearance that successive temporal stages of our life should appear as mutually exclusive. So McTaggart's account of the matter has some plausibility given the framework of his thought. We could not reasonably ask why a given person A should have fragmentary perceptions at all, in addition to the d.c. perceptions of the same objects: explanations have to stop somewhere, and he can as reasonably decline to answer as a Christian might decline to say why God created the world.

In giving this account of McTaggart's argument in 579–80 I have had to suppose that where McTaggart wrote '$G!H$' and '$c_xG!H$' this was a slip of the pen for 'G' and 'c_xG'. McTaggart frequently mentions $G!H$, G's d.c. perception of H, before and after the crucial passage; so such a slip of the pen would have been easy. In the footnote to 579 he explicitly tells us what he intends to talk about: 'I am here taking the whole content of the self at any one point in the series as forming one perception.' Now of course $c_xG!H$ does not contain the whole content of the person G at some stage of the C series, any more than $G!H$ contains the whole content absolutely of the person G. Nor does $G!H$ in any reasonable sense 'perceive', i.e. represent, itself; it is G's d.c. perception of another person H, and as such does not include G's perception of $G!H$; similarly, $c_xG!H$ cannot be said to 'perceive' itself. If we make my assumption about what McTaggart had in mind, all falls into place; for if G perceives himself, there will be a d.c. perception $G!G$ in which G perceives himself, and correspondingly there is a fragmentary perception $c_xG!G$ within the C-series stage c_xG, so that that very stage contains a representation of itself. By McTaggart's account, only by reason of the C stages' representing themselves can they *mis*represent themselves, and contrariwise he explicitly says that in a person who did not perceive himself a series of fragmentary misrepresentations could not exist (589).

To sum up: the slip I assume is psychologically a possible slip for an author to commit, as experience shows; it is even easy, if the author is copying for revision an extant M S of his own. And the emendation I propose makes good sense of McTaggart's argument. Broad has indeed attempted to expound the text just as it stands; but then he has to ascribe to McTaggart, in order to make the argument even look valid, tacit premises that he himself describes as fantastic, and which he has no special reason for ascribing to McTaggart apart from the exigences of interpretation. I see no need to discuss this matter further.

So far we have not considered the important question: what is the real ordering relation between the stages of perception represented by 'c_x', 'c_y'. They appear, as I said, separate from one another without overlap; but McTaggart holds this cannot be their real relation. The various C stages of a person's perception relate to the same field of objects: and they all fall within the person's several correct d.c. perceptions of the same objects; e.g. $c_xG!H$ within $G!H$, and $c_xG!K!H$ within $G!K!H$.

McTaggart now argues that $c_xG!H$ and $c_yG!H$, say, will both be states of misperception (*qua* parts of the states c_xG and c_yG, which misrepresent themselves as having separate content from G as a whole, and as being in time); but two states of misperception of H cannot, so to speak, pool their resources to make up a correct perception of H. c_xG and c_yG will represent one another as quite separate in content, and correspondingly will represent $c_xG!H$ and $c_yG!H$ (in introspection) as separate in content; but really this separateness of content cannot hold.

If $c_xG!H$ and $c_yG!H$, fragmentary and erroneous as they are, cannot separately go towards making up the complete d.c. perception $G!H$, the reason must be, McTaggart thinks, that one of them includes all the content of the other. So what appears as an order of perceptions of the object H falling outside one another in temporal succession is really a set of perceptions of H in which of any two, say $c_xG!H$ and $c_yG!H$, either the first is properly included in the second or the second in the first; and $G!H$ itself belongs to this 'inclusion series', including all other terms and included by none. The *terms* of the C series within any d.c. perception such as $G!H$ are then also terms of such an 'inclusion series'; and McTaggart forms the theory that the *ordering relations* are also the same. The order of the *C* series is of course the same as the apparent time-order; so McTaggart's theory is that if a term of the *C* series within *G!H* appears to occur temporally between two other terms, really this middle term includes one of the other terms and is included by the other. We have not yet considered whether the relations including/included correspond to the apparent temporal relations later/earlier, or rather to the relations earlier/later (558–61, 566).

I think McTaggart was here on to something very deep and important. It comes natural to us to represent successive temporal stages by successive and separate parts of a line; McTaggart would attribute this to the basic delusion whereby in each one of us the distinct *C* stages *misrepresent* each other as separated in content, not one including the other. But a number of thinkers have had the idea that inclusion (of the earlier stages by the later) is a better picture; and this idea has come to them quite apart from any suggestion that time is unreal – we find it for example in such champions of real change as William James (in *The Principles of Psychology*) and Bergson.

However, at this point as elsewhere McTaggart's pervasive tacit assumption that *part/whole* is a univocal relation puts his system under severe strain. If a body *A* is a proper part of a body *B*, there must be a remainder *E* that is added to *A* to make *B*. If then the *C* state $c_x G!H$ is properly included in $c_y G!H$, will there not be some residue which together with $c_x G!H$ constitutes $c_y G!H$? But there appears no place in McTaggart's system where such residues, considered as actual individual bits of a person's content, can possibly be fitted in. McTaggart explicitly denies that a person has any content except perceptions and grounds of perceptions (803), and on the other hand also denies that a less inclusive *C* stage $c_x G!H$ can go along with other perceptions to make a more inclusive stage $c_y G!H$. So if we conceived the increment by which the two differ as an individual entity, it could neither consist of perceptions nor yet have any other content. The only solution, I think, is to take seriously McTaggart's repeated statement that a less inclusive and a more inclusive *C*-stage differ in intensive magnitude. If a light grows brighter or a sound louder, it seems natural to say that the old light or sound is still there, with an increment; but we cannot treat the increment as an individual entity that has been added (568).

I conclude that we are not to conceive the more inclusive stages of a C series as containing the less inclusive *plus* individual increments, but simply as exceeding the less inclusive stages in respect of some intensive magnitude. Broad characteristically dreams up a very complicated theory in which there is *both* an increase of intensive magnitude *and* an individual entity identifiable as the addendum to $c_xG!H$ to make up $c_yG!H$; but we surely need not wish this theory on McTaggart. McTaggart's system is indeed put under some strain by admitting an inclusion-relation for which, unlike what holds for corporeal proper parts, there is no individual entity addible to the less inclusive to make the more inclusive; this may jeopardize reasonings earlier on, where the notions of whole and part, internal structure, etc. are unhesitatingly treated as univocal not analogical. But better this than outright contradiction. Our reading incidentally resolves an objection of Broad's that if $c_xG!H$ and $c_yG!H$ are not mutually exclusive, each might overlap the other without including it; such a relation of mutual overlap is manifest nonsense for intensive magnitudes, e.g. light and sound.

McTaggart uses an awkward and misleading terminology whereby he says that differences in intensive magnitude themselves have *extensive* magnitude (569). His reason is that these differences, unlike intensive magnitudes and like extensive magnitudes, can be added. An apter term had in fact already been devised by McTaggart's Cambridge contemporary W. E. Johnson; he called magnitudes of difference between intensive magnitudes '*distensive* magnitudes'. Distensive magnitudes really can be added: e.g. if we add the musical interval between C and D to the interval between D and E we get the interval between C and E. Distensive magnitudes are relational magnitudes, and addition corresponds not to putting together parts of a whole, but to the logicians' relative product (the relative product of the relations R and S is the relation of *being R to something that is S to* . . .). What makes it possible to add distensive magnitudes and compare them quantitatively is that *the same* difference in intensive magnitude may come at different points of a scale, e.g. one may go up by the musical interval of a fifth equally from a low note and from a high note.

McTaggart's doctrine is, then, that the more inclusive term $c_y G!H$ will differ from the less inclusive term $c_x G!H$ by an increased intensive magnitude. This intensive magnitude is necessarily one that we cannot perceive in present experience; for the nature of the time-delusion prevents us, as we have seen, from apprehending the real relation of inclusion between terms of the C series; we can only *infer that there is* an inclusion-relation, and that the more inclusive term includes the other term precisely by surpassing it in a certain intensive magnitude. (The question how we *can* be said to 'infer' this which we cannot perceive, when according to McTaggart there is no inference but only perception, has already been discussed in the chapter on Error; we saw there how McTaggart tried to reconcile the non-existence of inference with the patent fact that he himself had inferred that persons are timeless, and with the impossibility, on his own showing, of perceiving persons as timeless in present experience. As we saw, McTaggart attempted a solution: if this worked it would remove the present difficulty as well.)

It is of course not in principle any objection to a theory that it introduces a theoretically specified magnitude not accessible to direct observation. McTaggart tries to use the term 'amount of perception' for the magnitude here in question. Broad rightly objects that this term creates an illusion of our knowing which magnitude we are to have in mind. A more neutral term is to be found if we slightly adapt another piece of McTaggart's terminology. He speaks of the increments by which stages in a given series differ from one another as themselves forming a D series; but 'series' is here not to be taken very seriously, because he does not tell us what the ordering relation of the D series is supposed to be. Let us however adapt this term, and speak of the intensive magnitude that is greater in the more inclusive term of the C series as *D-magnitude*.

McTaggart remarks that distensive magnitudes, as we have agreed to call them, can serve in certain cases to give a numerical magnitude of intensive magnitudes. If we ignore complicated cases of non-Archimedean magnitudes, distensive magnitudes will be numerically comparable, not just addible, on condition that the same interval of qualitative difference is recognizable at different points of a linear scale. If the scale of intensive magnitudes has also a zero, a natural lower limit, then intensive magnitudes x and y may be numerically compared, via real numbers, by comparing the distensive magnitude of the gap between x and the zero with that of the gap between y and the zero. Thus in physics the thermodynamic measure of temperature works in this way: by reference to the working of an ideal heat engine, a temperature gap can be identified at different points of the temperature scale, as a musical interval can be at different points of the musical scale; and since we can describe a natural lower limit of temperature, the absolute zero, we can state a numerical ratio between two thermodynamic temperatures in terms of the ratio of the intervals between these temperatures and absolute zero.

Similarly, McTaggart holds, the D-magnitude of perceptions has an unattainable natural lower limit: nonentity, total absence of perception. The D-magnitude of $c_xG!H$ and $c_yG!H$ can in principle be numerically compared by comparing the distensive magnitude of the intervals between these D-magnitudes and mere impercipience. The difference in D-magnitude between $c_xG!H$ and $c_yG!H$ themselves is a natural measure of what appears *sub specie temporis* to be the time-interval between these stages. The importance of these considerations will be brought out further in the next chapter.

If we mentally review a C series in the direction from less inclusive to more inclusive terms, the D-magnitude of the terms increases, but we must not expect to find that this regularly goes with increases in the extent, accuracy, informativeness or clarity of the perceptions in the series. In present experience it seems to us that all these qualities of perception oscillate with time: we may e.g. have a clearer and more accurate perception coming temporally between two confused and inaccurate states of perception, or again a confused and inaccurate state of perception coming in between relatively clear and accurate ones. There is

F

not the faintest reason to doubt that the real C stages underlying temporal appearances actually are related in this way.

We shall presently consider McTaggart's view that the sense of the C series from less inclusive to more inclusive terms corresponds to the apparent earlier-to-later sense of the B series. But the increase in D-magnitude in this direction does not guarantee that *sub specie temporis* our perceptions will become steadily clearer, more accurate, etc. McTaggart insisted on this point, and did not let himself be fooled by his own talk about 'amount of perception' into believing the contrary. The like holds, he further insists, for qualities of life that we value, as well as these cognitive ones: virtue, happiness, love, emotional harmony, etc. All of these appear to wax and wane with time, and there is no reason to discount these appearances and regard any of these valuable qualities as increasing monotonically with D-magnitude of perception.

In the long run, indeed, C stages which are extremely inclusive, and then appear *sub specie temporis* as lying in the far future, may be expected to approximate closely to the complete d.c. perceptions, both in their cognitive and in their emotional features: they will still, however, be infected with the ubiquitous delusion of time. But that is very much of a long-term view and can give us little consolation for the present: the extreme difference in character, even in the best human life, between present experience and the d.c. perceptions as McTaggart describes them suggests a big difference in D-magnitude, and thus a wide apparent time-interval, 'between the present and that fruition'; and the prevalent fact of oscillation should increase our estimate of the time-interval.

We must now consider why McTaggart thought the 'less inclusive to more inclusive' sense of the C series was represented in our perception by the apparent earlier-to-later sense of the B series. He argues that the C series has a fundamental or more significant sense, because the relations of the fragmentary partial perceptions to the total d.c. perception of the same object are more significant than the relation of the perception to them. For example, the fragmentary parts have sufficient descriptions that are derived from those of d.c. perceptions; the d.c. perceptions can be sufficiently described with no mention of the fragmentary parts. The d.c. perceptions are correct, and the way they represent their objects does not require any special sort of misperception to be brought into its description; the fragmentary parts are various misperceptions of the same field of objects as is represented in the d.c. perceptions, and only by being variously erroneous do they differ from one another. Persons cannot exist, according to McTaggart, without having as content a system of d.c. perceptions that makes it possible for the content and internal structure of persons to satisfy the principles of sufficient description, ontological determinacy, and infinite differentiation into parts; there is no such way of showing that if persons exist fragmentary states of misperception must occur (717–22).

If in temporal appearance there were the same greater importance to be seen in the earlier-to-later sense of the *B* series as there is thus to be seen in the included-to-including sense of the *C* series, there would be, McTaggart argues, a strong reason for thinking that what thus appears to us as the fundamental sense of the *B* series is really the fundamental sense of the *C* series. Unfortunately McTaggart's main argument on this matter seems to me a complete failure. He argues that the earlier-to-later sense is the sense which in temporal appearance is fundamental, because this is the sense in which presentness appears to move (698). But all that amounts to, surely, is that first an earlier event appears to be present and then a later one; i.e. that *earlier* events appear to be present *earlier* than *later* ones. Why then by parity of reasoning should not the later-to-earlier sense be counted as fundamental, because *later* events appear to be present *later* than *earlier* ones?

McTaggart does better, I think, with a subsidiary argument, on which he dared not put too much stress for fear of being deceived by wishful thinking. Other things being equal, a man places more interest in his future than in his past: indeed, this greater interest of the future often outweighs the greater vagueness and uncertainty of our apprehension of it as compared with the past. Someone who looked back upon *n* years of misery and forward to *n* years of happiness would have a very different view of his life from someone who looked back upon n years of happiness and forward to n years of misery (701).

Some philosophers, particularly among those who like McTaggart have denied the reality of time, would hold such a difference in attitude to be irrational, and unworthy of a philosopher; he should regard good and evil in the apparent past and the apparent future as equally real and therefore equally important. McTaggart strongly disagreed. He would not condemn so ingrained a human attitude as irrational (703); and his own philosophy of time would perhaps supply it with a rational foundation, provided that what appears as the earlier-later relation is the relation of less inclusive to more inclusive states. Suppose that we have three C stages of a person G, c_xG, c_yG, and c_zG. Let the state c_xG be happy and state c_zG miserable. If the intermediate state c_yG is one that includes and so to say swallows up the miserable state c_zG, but itself is included in and swallowed up by the happy state c_xG, it is understandable that a blurred apprehension of the state of affairs, *sub specie temporis*, from the viewpoint of c_yG, in which c_zG appears as past and c_xG as future, should make c_xG itself a happy state. The reverse would hold if c_yG included and swallowed up the happy state c_xG but was itself included and swallowed up by the miserable state c_zG (726, 708–9).

McTaggart attached extreme importance to this matter. As we shall see in the next chapter, he thought that the Christian hope for a blessed eternal life in the future, although literally false (indeed internally contradictory, because what is eternal cannot be future), is as adequate an expression as popular thought can grasp of absolute reality: Heaven, he used to say, is as future as tomorrow's breakfast. Some superior persons (and they are still with us) deny the value of hope, not because the hope is vain in actual fact, but because a really wise and virtuous man will not set his heart on the future; McTaggart had no use for such an attitude (727–39).

There is a further difference between our apprehension of the past and the future: we apprehend the future in much less detail and with far less accuracy; there is no apprehension of the future that serves us as memory does, nor any reliable chronicle of the future fit to be compared even with the files of a newspaper. McTaggart intended to have utilized this fact towards developing his theory of how the relation included-inclusive appears as the earlier-later relation. But what we have in *The Nature of Existence* as it stands (678) is a mere hint, and I cannot do more than conjecture how McTaggart would have developed this hint if he had lived. As we saw, greater D-magnitude does not bring with it greater accuracy or clarity of perception, not by any general law; but McTaggart may have had a theory in mind about the nature of D-magnitude such that, if c_xG is less in D-magnitude than c_yG by the same amount as c_yG is less than c_zG, then (apart from countervailing factors) c_xG, which is already completely included in c_yG, will be more accurately represented in c_yG by way of 'memory' than c_zG is represented in c_yG by 'anticipation', when c_yG literally does not measure up to c_zG, having a small D-magnitude. I cannot do more than this by way of conjectural reconstruction. So striking an asymmetry between our apprehensions of the past and the future did not, as we see, escape McTaggart's notice; and he would doubtless have based some highly ingenious argumentation upon it if he had lived.

12 God, love, and Heaven

In his British Academy memoir of McTaggart, Broad has recounted that McTaggart enlivened College meetings because you never knew in advance what he was going to say. Fellows of Trinity thought in syndromes, and what they would say on questions that came up was drearily predictable; but McTaggart would use conventionally accepted premises and derive from them with apparently impeccable logic a highly unconventional conclusion, or contrariwise would defend a conventional position by arguments that embarrassed its supporters.

McTaggart's attitude in matters of religion showed this same characteristic independence of mind. He was an enthusiastic member of the Rationalist Press Association, but he thought and argued that a sound atheistic rationalist ought to defend the establishment and endowment of the Church of England. The wealth and prestige of that Church would produce enough envy, hatred, malice and all uncharitableness between it and other Christian denominations to prevent them from lining up together to stop the spread of atheism; and since the limits of orthodoxy and heresy in the Church of England are determined in the last resort, not by committed Christian theologians, but by lay lawyers concerned merely with a strict construction of the law, the Church would never become seriously and dangerously Christian. The argument is one that C. S. Lewis's devil Screwtape might use; but it has an undeniable force to justify McTaggart's unconventional attitude.

McTaggart's reasons for being an atheist were equally unusual and equally powerful. If we reject the reality of time – and as we saw it is very difficult to avoid contradiction if we do not – then, McTaggart argues, we must reject theism in its traditional

Jewish and Christian form. For in such theism an absolute distinction has to be made between the eternal unchangeable God and his mutable creatures: they depend upon God's will from moment to moment, and by that will could at any moment sink into nothingness. If we reject the reality of time, there cannot be this relation between God and creature, and therefore traditional theism must be rejected as false. On this issue, though I do not accept McTaggart's premise, his argument appears to me completely convincing given that premise. Some Christian apologists, like C. S. Lewis and Dorothy Sayers, have half-heartedly adopted the idea that time is unreal – unreal 'from God's point of view' – but only because their minds were less consequent than McTaggart's. And I think that to someone who in moments of reflection can *feel* the unreality of time as McTaggart could (see 501), the existence of the God of theism is simply incredible.

In *Some Dogmas of Religion* McTaggart considers certain deviant forms of belief in God, popular in some circles when he was writing. The idea of God as an all-inclusive person, one who somehow contained others as parts (an idea sometimes called *panentheism*) has never been prevalent in the West; no Christian denomination has adopted it. In *The Nature of Existence* McTaggart rejects panentheism on *a priori* grounds. On his view of persons, no two persons can have common parts at all; the parts of persons are their mental states, and no mental state can belong to more than one person; still less, then, can a person *A* be part of God, for then not some but all experiences that are parts of *A* would also be parts of God and among God's experiences (491).

McTaggart also considers the doctrine that there is a sort of finite God, a President of the Immortals rather than an absolute King. McTaggart regarded this idea as empirically unfounded and metaphysically uninteresting. According to his metaphysics, all persons are eternal, and there appear no grounds for ascribing higher ontological rank to one person than to another. As for one person's having power over others, the very idea must be a delusion of present experience. In absolute reality, a fulfilled will that so-and-so should be the case is simply an acquiescent perception of so-and-so as being the case, and this state of mind depends on the state of affairs perceived, not the other way round (495). It cannot be metaphysically interesting if one person merely *appears* to be pre-eminently powerful, like Hitler or Stalin; and McTaggart held that there is not even an empirical appearance of a cosmically powerful person. Such order and goodness as there appears to be in the Universe is sufficiently explained as the partly delusive appearance of the very great order and goodness that *must* exist in the Universe, because of the nature that absolute reality must have on pain of contradiction (499–500).

It may be of some interest to mention McTaggart's views on the problem of evil; he argued for these on grounds independent of his metaphysics. On the one hand, by implication he rejected the common argument that God is to blame because this is not the best of all possible worlds; the idea of a best possible world is incoherent, for there is no inherent upper limit to how good and happy a person can be, and even if there were one there could be more persons (814–16). On the other hand, the problem of evil arises already if there is a freely creative God; such a God is uniquely responsible for the world, and he can fail to bring about good or to eliminate evil only by not willing this (*DR* 182–90). Omnipotence, which for most people who have gone into the problem is the heart of the matter, appears to McTaggart a merely irrelevant topic; for absolute omnipotence, which can override logical contradictions, is an incoherent notion; and we need not discuss how omnipotent God is, if not absolutely omnipotent, because free power to create or not create already raises the essential difficulty.

It seems to me a pity that on these matters philosophers of religion have generally ignored McTaggart's views. It is anyhow a misconceived criticism on Broad's part to say that nobody really believes in an absolutely omnipotent God, so that McTaggart is knocking down a man of straw in refuting the view. At least one great philosopher, Descartes, argued for absolute omnipotence; and in teaching his philosophy to undergraduates, I have frequently encountered Evangelical Christians who thought Descartes was right. And I should agree with

McTaggart that popular religious argument often takes forms that would be defensible only if absolute omnipotence were assumed (*DR* 179).

McTaggart's metaphysics would guarantee, regardless of the existence of God, that the system of persons perceiving one another, what he called the d.c. system of perceptions, was a very good state: a timeless and endless state of love. Real assent to this doctrine, McTaggart thought, would be enough basis for a religion, and would make abandonment of belief in God something that we need not regret. Some people, indeed, would feel that religion was impossible and life meaningless without the love of God; but McTaggart thought they would live to get over this feeling. Love will not cease, and love is enough.

What then is the love of which McTaggart writes? Many writers of our time, so far from trying to make clear how they are using this most ambiguous word, seek rather to exploit its ambiguity. McTaggart made an exemplary effort to be clear. In the first place, only emotion felt towards an individual person is a case of love in his sense; highly as he valued patriotism, he did not call it *love* of one's country. Next, he distinguished love from both benevolence and sympathy. As he pointed out, you can sympathize with people's happiness or unhappiness even if you do not love them; and you can in fact feel a certain sympathy for those whom you hate, so long as the hatred is not too intense. And likewise general benevolence towards fellow-men, however active and passionate, is denied the name of love (459–60).

For McTaggart, love is a passionate liking for a person which is not *in respect of* his characteristics – except, perhaps, just the characteristic of being a person. I mentioned this idea of our emotion's being in respect of characteristics, when I was discussing McTaggart's view of how emotion depends upon cogitation. As we saw, he distinguished between having an emotion towards an object *O because of* a characteristic of *O*, and having an emotion towards *O in respect of* (what is cogitated as) a characteristic of *O*. Love, as McTaggart saw it, no doubt arose *because of* some special characteristic of the loved person, but was not felt *in respect of* such a characteristic (465).

McTaggart argues this point by remarking certain common

views we hold about love. We do not, he says, deprecate love if we regard it as having arisen from some trivial cause: if love does arise, it justifies itself, regardless of its cause. To love a woman faithfully all your life because of the way she looked when you first met is not made an unworthy thing because the occasion of falling in love was trivial. Nor do we deprecate love because it has no detectable cause. Admiration for a trivial reason, or for no detectable reason, is suspect or condemned; but then the reason for admiration of *B* is the characteristic *in respect of which* *B* is admired, whereas to give the cause of love is not to say *in respect of what* a person is loved (466).

Again, we should think it irrational to maintain admiration of a person in face of the discovery that the person was not as he was taken to be, courageous let us say, but just a cowardly braggart; and still more, if *C* admired *A* because of a mistake of identity whereby he confused *A* with *B*. But we do not think a man irrational in continuing to love a girl when he finds that she has not got some of the characteristics that originally formed part of her attractiveness for him. Even if *C* makes love to Miss *A* because he is short-sighted and mistakes her for Miss *B*, to whom he originally meant to propose, we do not say, if things go well between *C* and Miss *A*, that *C* has no right to this happiness, and ought to break off with Miss *A* and return to being a suitor of Miss *B*. However he has got there, *C* may be regarded as lucky (468).

It is no part of McTaggart's argument to say we are *right* in our approvals and disapprovals; he is concerned simply to explain our differing attitudes towards love and e.g. admiration; and he does this by saying that we implicitly recognize that love is an emotion towards a person *qua* person, not in respect of any characteristics. Where we disapprove e.g. of admiration, we disapprove of it as being in respect of characteristics that do not, to our mind, justify it. With love there is no question of characteristics, and thus no question of justification or non-justification.

Hatred is not in respect of characteristics either, as the rhyme 'I do not like thee, Dr Fell' testifies. In a curious footnote (468, n. 1) McTaggart alleges an asymmetry between our normal attitudes towards these polar opposites; but I think there is in fact perfect symmetry. Hatred is deplored, as love is welcomed, regardless of its cause; hatred would be excused, love condemned, only if felt towards an exceptionally vile object.

McTaggart regards it as a *sine qua non* condition of love that one should be specially conscious of union with another person. At this point there is a minor inconsistency. McTaggart holds that in absolute reality all persons love: but he also holds that there may be persons permanently deprived of self-consciousness. A person who was not self-conscious would *ipso facto* not be conscious of his own union with another person, and thus according to McTaggart's account of love would not have what it takes to be a lover. But I think the notion of a person who is not even potentially self-conscious is very dubious; McTaggart's defence of the notion appears unconvincing (397–8), and we could restore consistency by ascribing self-consciousness to all persons.

The inconsistency is clearly a result of McTaggart's never having given *The Nature of Existence* its final revision; the possibility of unself-conscious persons had been admitted in an earlier article on Personality that was incorporated bodily in the book. McTaggart elsewhere explains away our own apparent states of unself-consciousness by appealing to the theory of confused perception that we have already discussed (804–6). And any empirical evidence for the existence of permanently unself-conscious minds could be explained away similarly; such minds would simply be persons who in absolute reality perceive themselves, but who in present experience are in a state of very confused perception, in which self-consciousness never emerges from confused background perception.

To resume: An intense consciousness of union with another person is a necessary condition of love; McTaggart holds that if it is very intense, such consciousness is also a sufficient condition. Even if the characteristics of another person are very repellent, you must love him if you are sufficiently aware of your union with him; love is bound to arise, however torturing and destructive the love may be – cf. Baudelaire's *'C'est tout mon sang, ce poison noir!'* and Catullus' *'Odi et amo'*. McTaggart emphasizes that love neither seeks the beloved for the sake of happiness nor always finds happiness in the beloved; lovers would often forgo happiness rather than give up loving each other (468).

Now in the d.c. perceptions, each person perceives both himself and any other person whom he directly perceives, with complete clearness and distinctness. The consciousness A has of his union with a person B whom he directly perceives must be very much greater than any such consciousness of union can be under the conditions of confused and erroneous perception that we have in present experience; but sometimes even that is already sufficient for love. It follows that A's d.c. perception of B will certainly be a state of love. Moreover, for various reasons, which McTaggart spells out (473), this love will be much more intense than love ever is in present experience. First, there can, as we shall see, be no thwarted desire at the d.c. stage of perception. Again, the entire emotional life of every person, so far as concerns his d.c. perceptions, will be shown to flow from love. Again, it will be shown that various repellent characteristics of the beloved, which may have checked love in present experience, cannot do so here. Moreover, the d.c. perceptions not only are eternal, but represent their objects as being eternal; so love is enhanced by the consciousness that it will never end, that it is here to stay. Finally, the consideration that for McTaggart was most important of all: the greater intimacy of d.c. perception is of itself a guarantee, not only that there will be love, but that it will be far more intense than our present love (473).

The argument that among the d.c. perceptions there can be none that are thwarted desires on their volitional side is quite straightforward. A thwarted desire involves simultaneously cogitating an object A as being X and as not being X; A must be cogitated as being X, a cogitation coloured with desire, and at the same time as not being X, so that the desire is thwarted. For McTaggart, there are no forms of cogitation really except perception; so thwarted desire, which involves an object's being cogitated as X and as not being X, must involve misperception. (I argued earlier that such misperception of an object as having incompatible characteristics does actually occur; an Escher engraving enables us to *see* an impossible state of affairs.) But among the d.c. perceptions there are no misperceptions; so there can be no thwarted desires there (452, cf. 683).

It follows that none of the d.c. perceptions can be coloured by emotions that involve thwarted desire and could check or prevent love: anger, hatred, jealousy, fear, envy, malice. Fear, along with hope, is excluded also on another count – by the absence of the delusion of time. One emotion that has been counted (e.g. by Moore) as a great intrinsic evil is not mentioned by McTaggart: lasciviousness. But this emotion involves, in McTaggart's theory, the misperception of a person as corporeal, and therefore cannot colour the correct d.c. perceptions. The proof that these disturbing features must be absent from the d.c. perceptions depends solely on the absence of error, not on the presence of love; this both removes a *prima facie* objection to McTaggart's thesis that the intimacy of d.c. perception must bring love with it, and justifies his reasoning that love, freed from such disturbances, must be far more intense than in our present life (478–80).

The other emotions that colour d.c. perceptions are all dependent on love. Each of us will regard himself with what McTaggart calls self-reverence (477); he will feel himself king and God because he loves. (To my mind this is a pleasanter idea of self-reverence than Kant's idea of revering oneself as a promulgator of the moral law; it certainly answers to a lot of what poets say.) People whom we do not directly perceive, but only perceive as mirrored in other people's perceptions of them, we shall not regard with love, because we shall have less consciousness of unity with them than with our beloved; but we shall regard them with a lesser degree of liking which may be suitably called affection – such an emotion as we feel, or tend to feel, in present experience towards people who are loved or even liked by those we love. In present experience indeed this tendency may be checked by the repulsive characteristics of the one our beloved favours, or again by jealousy; but such checks are excluded from the d.c. perceptions (475).

The mental states of people whom we love we shall regard

with no vain wish that they should be otherwise: rather, with what McTaggart calls acquiescence – active acceptance. Even the pains and sorrows, the errors and wickedness, found in the pre-final stages of those we love, and of ourselves who love them, will in the final stage be regarded with active acceptance: for we shall perceive them correctly, perceive them as constituent parts necessary to the existence of those who love and are loved, and just this will determine our acquiescence. Towards all the evils of present experience we shall have an *O felix culpa* attitude (894–7).

When McTaggart thus regards all the evils of present life as having been taken into a wider whole and their evils neutralized, I cannot help suspecting a Hegelian hangover in his thought. Hegel is notorious for his use of the participle '*aufgehoben*', which like Latin '*sublatus*' may mean either 'raised up higher' or 'taken away': I am afraid McTaggart had some such double-faced notion of what happens to present evils of misperception when considered as fragmentary parts of the correct d.c. perceptions.

The system of d.c. perceptions constitutes a *final* stage of the Universe and of all persons in the Universe. As we saw, in any given C series falling wholly within some one d.c. perception, this d.c. perception itself stands to each of the fragmentary perceptions of the same object in the very relation – *differing by having a greater D-magnitude* – that the 'later' stages of the C series bear to the 'earlier' ones. The final state of love, which McTaggart also calls Heaven, is in his words 'as really future as tomorrow's breakfast'. Tomorrow's experiences stand to today's experiences in the relation of being got from them by an increase of D-magnitude, and Heaven stands in the very same relation to tomorrow's and today's experiences, a relation systematically misperceived as the relation of later to earlier. So if we wish to think with the learned but speak with the vulgar, we shall say that Heaven is in the future, to be regarded with joyful and confident expectancy (727–37).

Christians have in fact often said simultaneously that Heaven is a state of the soul, that Heaven is future, and that Heaven is eternal. McTaggart holds that his philosophy alone can show the meaning and the truth of this claim. Time is a delusion, so there is nothing for Heaven to be but eternal; but Heaven has that relation to our present experiences which makes us call to-morrow's experiences future; and Heaven is a spiritual state, since only spirits exist (738–9).

Of course, from the heavenly point of view, the experiences that constitute our present misperceptions are also timeless and eternal; but since everything appears in Heaven as it really is, A's states of misperception are perceived in Heaven as states that *appear to themselves*, from their own point of view, to be transitory; whereas Heaven appears in Heaven, not only as an eternal state, but as a state *correctly representing itself* as eternal.

What about the stages in between the present and Heaven? To parody Browning:

> There must be Heaven; there is no Hell;
> Meanwhile there is our life here. Well?

According to McTaggart, the series of a man's experiences neither began with birth (nor even in the womb – cf. Descartes' speculations about an obscure pre-natal consciousness) nor will end with death. On the contrary, increments in D-magnitude of perception are the foundation in absolute reality for the appearance of temporal intervals; and thus for any given C series we have (617–19):

$$\frac{\text{Apparent time between } c_x G\,!H \text{ and } c_y G\,!H}{\text{Apparent time between } c_w G\,!H \text{ and } c_z G\,!H} =$$

$$\frac{\text{Increment in } D\text{-magnitude of perception from } c_x G\,!H \text{ to } c_y G\,!H}{\text{Increment in } D\text{-magnitude of perception from } c_w G\,!H \text{ to } c_z G\,!H}$$

This objective foundation for time measurements enables us to make temporal correlations between C series in different persons. For all C series have a common lower limit in non-entity, zero perception; and if the increments needed to reach $c_x G\,!H$ and $c_y K\,!L$ from zero are alike x per cent of the increments that are needed to reach $G\,!H$ and $K\,!L$ themselves from zero, then *sub specie temporis* $c_x G\,!H$ and $c_y K\,!L$ are simultaneous – they are each separated from what appears as the beginning of time, a state of zero perception, and each separated from Heaven, which appears as the end of time, by equal time-stretches. Each person's history thus stretches right through the history of the Universe (615–16, 620, 759).

It seems to follow that most likely each person has a plurality of lives. At certain intervals along a person's C series there is a total loss of memory and a sinking of his consciousness to the state of confused apprehension of things that exists in baby-hood. From this dramatic oscillation, where we lose much in clarity and accuracy of perception (though *not*, McTaggart holds, in its 'amount' in the technical sense) there is a very rapid recovery; there follows a long stretch of comparatively clear and accurate perception; then, quickly or slowly, we relapse again into confusion and error.

An obvious objection to plurality of lives is that loss of memory involves loss of personal identity. McTaggart had little esteem for Locke's theory that personal identity involves memory; but in any event he could answer Locke on Locke's own ground. In Heaven there is clear and distinct perception of all the pre-final stages just as they were – or rather, just as they unchange-ably *are*. Of course in Heaven these stages are not misperceived as past and gone, which is the way that our present memories misrepresent pre-final stages; but pre-final stages will, quite correctly, be perceived in Heaven as stages which *appear to them-selves* as transitory and appear in other pre-final stages as past. So it will not be too misleading to say that in Heaven all pre-final stages are perfectly remembered. Now nobody thinks that temporary loss of memory, followed by complete recovery, counts against personal identity; so even though the pre-final part of a person's C series consists of many lives, with loss of memory at the end of each, the recovery of memory in Heaven shows that even on Locke's view there is no loss of personal identity (767–70).

Even so, we may be worried by the recurrent loss that this repeated regression to infantile confusion may mean to us. McTaggart would sternly insist that if our reason shows the world to involve such a fact, we must accept it as a fact, however grim it seems. However, he argues that we need not find this fact very grim. Even though our actual memories of events in our previous lives will be gone, we may reasonably expect that aptitudes of mind acquired in one life will carry on to the next: someone who has no conscious memory of mathematics, let us say, will recover lost ground with extreme rapidity once he has mathematical textbooks in his hand to revive his memory. This is how McTaggart explains 'innate' intellectual aptitudes (755: DR 95–6, 104). Similarly, 'innate' virtuous (or vicious) tendencies would be the effect of habits acquired in a previous life (776: DR 95–6, 105).

At *every* stage of the C series, a person A perceives everybody whom A perceives, and therefore loves, in Heaven. Of course A's perception of B in present experience is incomparably less clear and correct than A's d.c. perception of B in Heaven; and the degree of misperception in such a state, say $c_x A!B$, may be so great that B is not recognized as a person at all; or even if B is so recognized, B's characteristics may be so misrepresented that the state $c_x A!B$ is not a state of love or is even a state of hatred. However, if there is love in the heavenly d.c. perception $A!B$, it is incredible that *no* pre-final stage, however little different in D-magnitude of perception from $A!B$, should be a state of love; and however much oscillation there may be, if there is love of A for B in the final stage, this love must occur and recur in the pre-final stages, and must in the long run grow and grow, and recur more and more often. There may, however, be absences and estrangements, because oscillation is so pervasive a feature of the pre-final stages. But when the lover sees all perfection in his mistress, and the cynical world laughs at his delusion, McTaggart holds that it is the world, not the lover, that is sunk deep in delusion; the lover perceives by anticipation the real beauty that he will see face to face in Heaven (DR 232).

Is there anything to mar the perfection of Heaven? McTaggart thinks there can be one thing: pain. Heaven excludes the pain of frustration and revolt; but he holds there can be an acquiescent pain, independent of thwarted desire. In Heaven there will be a completely detailed and accurate perception of all the sorrow, misery, and rage in the pre-final stages; will not this produce reverberations of pain – what McTaggart calls sympathetic pain – in the final stage itself?

At this rate the final stage might indeed be a state of profound love, but also one of profound unhappiness; love does not exclude unhappiness. McTaggart sought to eliminate this threat to the happiness of Heaven by long and elaborate arguments about values (786–903). I think, however, that it is logically unnecessary to go into value theory at all at this point. All we need is a premise which McTaggart would certainly have asserted: that *at* the final stage the hedonic effect – the effect on pleasure and pain – of any finitely long stretch of the *C* series, in which the stages appear from their own point of view as transitory, is *less* than the hedonic effect of perceptions *of* the final stage itself, which not only is, but appears to itself as, eternal and non-transitory. So far as one can speak of probabilities in such obscure regions, the premise appears plausible; delusions which represent *themselves* as transient will in Heaven have an insignificant effect on our happiness, as compared with the d.c. perception of the blessed and self-consciously eternal state of Heaven itself. And this preserves the spirit, if not the letter, of McTaggart's argument in the crucial sections 898–902.

In this book, the value theory developed in this long segment of *The Nature of Existence* calls for no detailed discussion. Here and there there are important points made, most of which have been picked up in this commentary. But the main lines of McTaggart's value theory are not original. Like many Cambridge men of his generation, he was profoundly impressed by a profoundly confused book: G. E. Moore's *Principia Ethica*. When you have read that, you have really learned all that McTaggart has to say about good and evil, intrinsic value, and the like; but for those who desire to explore these mirky regions I have given the section reference. We need not discuss value theory. We have before us McTaggart's account of how the Universe is, and must be, constituted: whether we like such a world or not, whether we think it good or bad.

The influence of *Principia Ethica* is an extraordinary phenomenon in the history of English philosophy. Cambridge men of that generation really thought (I can remember my father continuing to think) that now for the first time in the history of philosophy ethics had been given a really rigorous foundation. This was Moore's own claim; the wonder is that men like Russell, McTaggart and Maynard Keynes accepted it. McTaggart incorporated a mini-treatise *à la* Moore on value theory into *The Nature of Existence*; Russell wrote another, *The Elements of Ethics*, on the same lines (though he was soon to recant); Lord Keynes has told us how a whole circle was possessed with the idea that the whole duty of man was to secure valuable experiences, chiefly aesthetic and erotic ones. Clive Bell's *Civilization* is another document of the same period and spirit. I do not think any competent logician who scrutinized Moore's argument would consider it rigorous nowadays.

Though optimistic, McTaggart's conclusions were not cheaply and easily optimistic. He insists over and over again that the existence of evil in our world is not delusory; it cannot be an error that there is unhappiness (857), nor, obviously, that there is error (510); and in general a delusion that so effectively hid the goodness of the world from us, if in fact the world were unmixedly good, would be a great evil (857: *DR* 171). Nor does he try to conceal or to explain away the fact that there are very great evils in present experience. Further, he thought that in the world-long life each of us has before him, there may very well be 'delusions, crimes, sufferings, hatreds', far surpassing what we have known up to now; and there is not the faintest reason to expect steady progress; even *long* periods of deterioration, for the individual and for the world as a whole, cannot be excluded (784, 907–10). All that McTaggart's philosophy can say to console us is that our present sufferings and sins and errors will in Heaven appear infinitely insignificant (913):

And thus the very greatness of evil which we endure gives us some slight anticipation of the greatness of the good which outweighs it infinitely.

Of the nature of that good we know something. We know that it is a powerful and endless state of love – love so direct, so intimate, and so powerful that even the deepest mystic rapture gives us but the slightest foretaste of its perfection. We know that we shall know nothing but our beloved, and those they love, and ourselves as loving them, and that only in this shall we seek and find satisfaction. Between the present and that fruition there stretches a future which may well need courage. For while there will be in it much good, and increasing good, there may await us evils which we can now measure only by their infinite insignificance as compared with the final reward (913).

This is the life everlasting in which McTaggart believed, firmly and as he thought rationally. Of course a man must test and test again the conclusions of his reason; but having reached some conclusion that on rational grounds seems unshakably certain, he ought to hold to this, and not abandon it because the events of his private life or of recent history make it seem 'too good or too bad to be true' (*DR* 59). Some people think an 'agonizing reappraisal' of dogmas is called for in an age that has seen the tyrannies of Stalin and Hitler; but these more recent evils cannot upset any dogma that was compatible with the careers of Tamerlane and Shaka Zulu and Lopez of Paraguay. To let the emotional impact of what is near to us in space and time determine our view of the world as a whole is quite irrational; to publish pretended justifications for such an abandonment of reason is contemptible.

McTaggart was a very different sort of man: one of those who firmly 'resolve that, so far as their strength may prevail, neither the pains of death nor the pains of life shall drive them to any comfort in that which they hold to be false, or drive them from any comfort in that which they hold to be true' (*DR* 59). And he died as he had lived:

> One who never turned his back but marched breast forward,
>   Never doubted clouds would break,
> Never dreamed, though right were worsted, wrong would
>   triumph,
> Held we fall to rise, are baffled to fight better,
>   Sleep to wake.[1]

---

[1] Browning, Epilogue to *Asolando*

Bibliographical note

McTaggart's works

Studies in the Hegelian Dialectic. Cambridge University Press, 1896.

Studies in Hegelian Cosmology. Cambridge University Press, 1901.

Some Dogmas of Religion. London: E. Arnold, 1906: second printing, with an introduction by C. D. Broad, 1930.

A Commentary on Hegel's Logic. Cambridge University Press, 1910.

Human Immortality and Pre-existence. London: E. Arnold, 1916.

The Nature of Existence, vol. 1. Cambridge University Press, 1921; vol. 2, edited by C. D. Broad, Cambridge University Press, 1927.

Philosophical Studies, edited with an introduction by S. V. Keeling. London: E. Arnold; New York: Longmans, Green, 1934. (A collection of articles.)

Works about McTaggart

Broad, C. D. *Examination of McTaggart's Philosophy.* Cambridge University Press; vol. 1, 1933; vol. 2 (printed as two volumes), 1938.

Dickinson, G. Lowes. *J. McT. E. McTaggart.* (With chapters by Basil Williams and S. V. Keeling.) Cambridge University Press, 1931.

McTaggart's MSS

McTaggart wrote five complete drafts of every book published in his lifetime: Drafts A, B, C, D, and E. The only surviving MSS that I have been able to find are in Trinity College, Cambridge, in the Wren Library: a complete Draft A of vol. 2 of *The Nature of Existence*, together with some notes made for the preparation of Draft B.

In his editorial preface to the printed version of this volume, Broad states that he prepared it from Draft C up to Section 567, p. 241, and thereafter from Draft B. These MSS have not been found among Broad's papers. Death prevented McTaggart's doing any further drafts.

Index